Bir Hacheim: desert citadel

Bir Hacheim: desert citadel

Richard Holmes

Editor-in-Chief: Barrie Pitt
Editor: David Mason
Art Director: Sarah Kingham
Picture Editor: Robert Hunt
Designer: Barry Miles
Cover: Denis Piper
Special Drawings: John Batchelor
Photographic Research: Colette Dumez
Cartographer: Richard Natkiel

Ballantine Books Inc.
101 Fifth Avenue New York NY 10003

An Intext Publisher

Contents

Revival of a Nation

"LE MONDE A RECONNU LA FRANCE QUAND, À BIR-HAKIM, UN RAYON DE SA GLOIRE RENAISSANTE EST VENU CARESSER LE FRONT SANGLANT DE SES SOLDATS"

GÉNÉRAL de GAULLE
CHEF DES FRANÇAIS LIBRES
LONDRES, LE 18 JUIN 1942

Introduction by Kenneth Macksey

The defence of Bir Hacheim in June 1942 by General Koenig's 1st Free French Brigade marked the turning point in the fortunes of de Gaulle and the Free French organisation he had brought painfully and rebelliously into being in June 1940. At the beginning the Free French had suffered by reason of their meagre resources and low political standing: two years later, after Bir Hacheim, their voices were loud and influential.

The crushing of France by the Germans in 1940, after a lightning campaign, represented one of the most shattering débâcles in French history. One day the nation seemed to stand confidentially among the greatest military powers in Europe; the next she lay defenceless and prostrate. Not only were her armed forces vanquished, but her spirit was broken. Strong Frenchmen wept, but precious few contemplated a continuation of the struggle. Those who, like temporary Brigadier-General Charles de Gaulle, determined to fight on were branded by the Vichy Government, under Marshal Pétain, as renegades. In June de Gaulle might declaim that 'There is no France without a sword', and set his face against Frenchman bearing arms against Frenchman. But inevitably, in treading the path towards his political goal of a unified France, he steered a course leading in the direction of tragedy before triumph. The bloodless coups in West and Central Africa would be followed by fratricide at Dakar and in Syria, along with a wide schism dividing those who spoke for France from within and those who laid claims from abroad. De Gaulle's fervid and resolute advocacy of the integrity and future influence of France would be raised amid clouds of pride, passion and exhortation, and create in the minds of his allies the appearance of hopeless intransigence.

Yet de Gaulle, groping towards the ultimate power which more than a decade later was to be his, foresaw the future more clearly than did many of his contemporaries – and saw it all the better because he possessed an idealised faith. Though, in the USA, the State Department might denigrate de Gaulle, and Roosevelt might later liken him in jest to Joan of Arc, France certainly needed her Joan after 1940. If Churchill bridled at the brusque independence of the Frenchman he had helped (as a poor second choice) into power, he nevertheless sensed the man's destiny as well as the political importance of the Free French organisation. And though the British people might be disillusioned by the French (as the French felt deserted by the British) they hesitated to reject France, for in de Gaulle they saw a friend as well as a symbol because he lived among them and took their cause at a time of stress.

Early in 1942, however, the Gaullist cause was faded. It had taken knocks, suffered too many rebuffs, and expressed itself by an excess of high words not matched by resounding deeds. The Free French urgently needed a victory of their own to demonstrate their true claim to be Fighting French. It is unlikely, however, that they dreamed of such glory as came with the posting of Koenig's Brigade in the isolated fortress of Bir Hacheim. For let it be remembered that in May the hopes of the British Eighth Army, in the Western Desert, were based upon their offensive starting before that of the Axis. Only because they lost that race did the circumstances arise whereby the French were attacked and compelled to execute a desperate stand in supreme isolation.

For the defence of Bir Hacheim was French in spirit and the author of this book, Richard Holmes, a francophile, paints a picture of France's traditional courage and determination at its best. He talks of individuals, who rose above the crowd, and of the cosmopolitan character of Koenig's force – men from all over the French Empire and from without, men of all colours too, some of them German who were fated to oppose their own countrymen, disciplined by a system to put loyalty to the French Foreign Legion before country. Yet the fires of patriotism were at the root of the sixteen-day defence, for as the author says, 'If Koenig's men had failed to do all that could be expected of them, then the death knell of the French army would have tolled for the second time in two years'. Then, too, he might have added, France could have forfeited all hope of credibility as a force in the councils of nations for generations to come. At any rate the chances of de Gaulle walking to Notre Dame in glory in August 1944 might well have been expunged.

It is perhaps significant that Richard Holmes, whose present interest in France centres upon the study of the failing Second Republic, should write about Bir Hacheim, for in a sense it was this battle which made possible the Fifth Republic whose strength gave France greater unity than at any time in her history since Napoleon departed for Elba.

The fall of France

At 0430 hours on 18th May 1940 the German tanks of 1st Panzer Division rattled across the Luxembourg frontier, spearheading the third German invasion of France in sixty years. The campaign that followed gave a practical demonstration of the fury of Blitzkrieg to an astonished Europe. In only six weeks, Northern and Central France were submerged beneath a *feldgrau* flood. The British, French and Belgian armies, fighting with varying degrees of skill and enthusiasm, were harried by aircraft, mauled by armour, and driven from the field. The fall of France seemed sudden, unexpected, and, in immediate restrospect at least, irreversible. Yet the history of the interwar years demonstrates that the events of 1940 had logical antecedents. Furthermore, the course of the war was to prove that the catastrophe of 1940, great though it was, was not determinate.

The grand victory parade that flowed, behind squealing trumpets, down the *Champs-Elysées* on 14th July 1919 was little more than a gaudy cloak to grim facts. For the previous four years France had been bled white. Well over 1,000,000 of her soldiers had died on the muddy plains of Flanders, the broken uplands of the Argonne or the rolling chalk slopes of Champagne. Still more had been wounded, and many of them were confined for ever to the painful and unproductive monotony of hospital life. The French economy had suffered appallingly. Northern France had been ravaged; towns, roads and railways had been destroyed, and an alarming decline in industrial production worsened a growing trade deficit.

Hopes that the financial ills of France would be cured by a rapid injection of money from the defeated Germany proved woefully vain. Germany too had suffered terribly during the war, and was unable to meet Allied demands for reparations. When, in 1923, Germany failed to pay up, French troops occupied the Rhineland in an effort to compel her to do so. Far from producing the desired effect, this show of force simply knocked the remaining props from under the tottering German economy. The ensuing financial collapse within Germany heightened German bitterness towards France, and was instrumental

14th July 1919. Joffre and Foch parade victoriously in Paris

in facilitating the rise of the Nazi Party Deteriorating Franco-German relations unfolded across a gloomy international scene. America, regretting the impulses which had brought her into the war, retreated steadily into isolationism and preoccupation with her own problems. Britain, too, with nearly 1,000,000 dead, and economic crises of her own, had little desire to incur any new involvement in Europe.

Within France, the euphoria of victory did not long survive the war's conclusion. Prompted by fears of the Bolshevik menace, the parties of the Right combined to form the *Bloc National Republicain,* which successfully held its own against an increasingly fragmented Left. The governments in the prewar Third Republic had never been noted for their stability; after 1918, too, ministry continued to follow ministry with cyclical predictability. Ideals, causes, and, above all, leaders, were lacking. The men who should have replaced the rejected Clemenceau or the ageing Poincaré had been killed during the war, or had returned from the front, numb with horror, unwilling or unable to inject any fire or idealism into the conduct of government. Politicians squabbled about whose turn it was for office, and earned for the Third Republic the well-merited sobriquet 'Republic of Pals'. There were, as de Gaulle pointed out, 'men of inestimable value and sometimes of great talent . . . But the political game consumed them and paralysed them.'

If the cold breath of the dead chilled the hearts of French statesmen, it also infused her military leaders with an overwhelming desire to prevent any recurrence of the muddy calamities of the First World War. In 1914 the French army had stormed forward imbued with the confidence of *l'offensive à l'outrance* – which had nearly resulted in France's losing the war in the first month. As the doctrine of the

General Philippe Pétain in 1916

blind offensive had prevailed before 1914, so, conversely, the strategy of rigid defence reigned after 1918. To many French soldiers, the traumatic experience of Verdun exemplified the advantages of the defensive battle, and epitomised French courage, determination and stoicism. Before 1914 the French soldier had all too often envisaged himself as a figure by Vernet or Detaille – bronzed, mustachioed and impeccably tailored. Such illusions were no longer possible in the aftermath of the First World War. The élan of the old army had died with a flicker of white gloves in August 1914, and a series of costly offensives in the four years that followed buried it beyond hope of resurrection.

The doctrine of the 'continuous front' took shape gradually in the 1920s, aided by the presence of Marshal Pétain, revered defender of Verdun, as Inspector-General of the Army. The logic behind the doctrine was clear enough. Hundreds of thoussands of French infantrymen had died trying to hold a line of badly-dug, bitterly uncomfortable trenches, stretching in a painful line from Switzerland to the North Sea. The best way to avoid a recurrence of this tragic situation was, argued the theorists, to construct a permanent fortified line – a 'continuous front' of immense strength against which any German assault must surely fail. This French version of the Great Wall of China was sanctioned by the National Assembly early in 1930, and took its name from a veteran of the First World War, who happened to be Minister of War at the time – André Maginot.

The Maginot Line, despite the opprobrium now adhering to its name, must be reckoned as one of the masterpieces of military architecture. It was designed to run from the Swiss frontier to Longwy on the Belgian border.

Verdun 1916, the 'mincing machine' which bled France white and changed French strategy between the wars from the offensive to the defensive

13

Exterior and interior of the Maginot
Line, the concrete realisation of the
doctrine of the 'continuous front'
which was dominant in the 1920s

An extension of the line along the
Belgian border itself was believed to
be unnecessary and impolitic; it
would increase the already crippling
cost of the line, and could not fail to
alienate the Belgians, who were, at
the time of the line's commencement,
allied to France. The strongest por-
tions of the Maginot Line lay across
the two main invasion routes, and
covered the Metz-Nancy area and
lower Alsace. Defences were sited in
depth. A double line of wire, anti-tank
obstacles and pillboxes was designed
to slow down the attacker; behind
this barrier lay a network of underground casemates and forts. The forts
themselves were impressive in the
extreme. They contained barracks,
railways, airconditioning plants and
power stations, and powerful guns.

The imposing facade of the line
concealed numerous deadly weak-
nesses. The line failed to cover the
Belgian frontier, the classical route to
'the pit of the French stomach'. It
was, furthermore, only partially completed owing largely to financial
considerations. Finally, the men who
garrisoned the subterranean strong-
points were too few, and in many
senses too feeble, for their task.
Compulsory military service had long
been the *bête noir* of the Left, and
political pressure had resulted in its
reduction from three years to one.
The manpower ratio between France
and Germany was well over 1:3 in
favour of the latter. Coupled with
this drastic shortage of personnel
was the army's lack of mission. The
old goal of *revanche* had been achieved.
The lost provinces of Alsace and
Lorraine were in French hands once
more. French officers trailed their
sabres over the cobblestones of Metz,
and the streets of Strasbourg were
alive with *bleu horizon*. *La gloire* had
made its final exit from French
military life, but had not been replaced by more mundane considerations. Army pay was abysmally low –
but was no lower than the social
standing of the army officer.

Assailed by the Left, with low pay
and dwindling social status, many
officers sought refuge in extreme

General Gamelin, Inspector-General of the Army after 1935 and vigorous proponent of the 'ideas of 1918'

Pétain, whose influence remained colossal even after he handed over the leadership to Weygand in 1930

Right-wing – even neo-Fascist – political movements. Both Charles Maurras' *Action Française* and Colonel de la Rocque's *Croix de Feu* had a sizeable following amongst the cadres. For the ranks, though, the other side of the political coin had its attractions; the reports of the army's Intelligence Service noted an alarming increase of Communism within the army.

Many of the army's failings could be attributed to its leadership. At the head of the army stood the men of 1918. Pétain's influence was colossal, even after 1930 when he handed over leadership to his disciple Weygand. Gamelin, who took over in 1935, drew such popularity as he possessed from his rôle in the battle of the Marne twenty-one years before. It is scarcely remarkable that the tactics of 1918 became enshrined in French tactical doctrine, just as the doctrine of defence had become the cornerstone of French strategy. The terrain-

firepower concept prevailed. If an advance had to be made, then it would follow the established principle that 'artillery conquers, infantry occupies'. A jaundiced observer at a military exercise in 1936 noted the elaborate attention paid to supporting an advance with fire, and commented drily that 'at the rate of 1,500 metres a day, it will take us some time to reach Berlin.'

Obsolescent weapons vied with obsolete doctrine to obstruct military progress. French views on the tactical employment of armoured vehicles, while not unique, were sadly outmoded, and were to prove a major factor in the defeat of 1940. The French regarded the tank as, primarily, a mobile pillbox, whose main function was infantry support. In 1921 Pétain had decreed that 'Tanks assist the advance of the infantry by breaking static obstacles and active resistance put up by the enemy.' There were those who found such views unsatisfactory. In Britain, Captain Basil Liddell Hart propounded the theory that an 'expanding torrent' of tanks, backed up by mobile infantry and artillery, was the key to success in future war.

Variations on this theme found support within certain sections of the French army. In 1935, Major Charles de Gaulle, in his book *Vers l'armée de métier*, gave a balanced assessment of France's security problem, and suggested a solution. France, maintained de Gaulle, was by reason of her geography, and the very nature of the French and German peoples, always open to a sudden attack. To meet this threat, he advocated the formation of six highly mobile divisions, each with a large proportion of armour, plus one light division, backed by an army reserve of tanks and heavy guns. The entire force would number about 100,000 men, who, de Gaulle insisted, should all be professional soldiers.

The publication of de Gaulle's book lent fuel to the literary battle which was already blazing. The scattered parties of the Left had solidified, temporarily at least, into the *Front Populaire*, whose leader, Léon Blum, saw a professional army as a danger to the republic. More rational considerations allied with Blum's doctrinaire arguments in opposing a sudden change in defence policy. General Maurin, who succeeded Pétain as Minister of War, warned of the danger in changing strategic doctrine in midstream, as it were. 'When we have devoted so many efforts to building up a fortified barrier', declaimed Maurin, 'is it conceivable that we would be mad enough to go ahead of this barrier into I know not what adventure?' Thus, for both political and military reasons, a professional army and a mechanised striking force were damned - and with them, France's last hope of resisting the growing menace across the Rhine.

The German occupation of the Rhineland, on 7th March 1936, illus-

Léon Blum, the French Prime Minister. He opposed a change to a more offensive strategy

trated the flaws in the French military machine. General Gamelin, eager to avoid responsibility for decision-making, grossly overemphasised German strength, and gloomily prophesied that French intervention in the Rhineland would require general mobilisation. This was politically unacceptable; elections were near, and no politician could face conscripting his voters. While France hesistated, the resurgent – but dangerously weak – Wehrmacht entered the Rhineland unopposed.

The Treaty of Versailles, which ended the First World War, had imposed certain restrictions upon the military forces of the defeated Germany. German compliance with these clauses had never been more than half-hearted. By the end of 1933 the treaty-imposed limit of 100,000 men was a thing of the past. In March 1935 all pretence was laid aside. Hitler announced the foundation of a new German army with a peacetime

strength of thirty-six divisions. This figure rose steadily; by 1937 there were thirty-nine divisions, and, two years later, fifty-one. This rapid expansion took place around the nucleus of General Hans von Seeckt's 100,000-man Reichswehr, Germany's élite, highly professional interwar army. Perhaps the most alarming thing about the Wehrmacht was not so much its size, but the emphasis it placed upon up-to-date techniques. Liddell Hart's ideas had found attentive ears in Germany. In 1937 a German officer, Heinz Guderian, published *Achtung-Panzer*, which sketched out the use and composition of the armoured division, and was not least among the blueprints of Blitzkrieg. French antimilitarism and apathy was matched, in Germany, by a fervent desire for revenge and by what Guderian termed 'a fanatical will to move forward'. Europe spun steadily down the long smooth groove leading to disaster.

Léon Blum's Popular Front found its path unexpectedly rough. A rash of strikes broke out on the heels of Blum's success at the polls. These were terminated by the Matignon agreement – a remarkably far-sighted piece of industrial legislation – but the problems of the Popular Front did not end there. The economy continued its downward spiral, and Blum was forced to devalue the franc. While German industrial production, particularly of armaments, continued to rise, that of France reached a new low ebb. This, not unnaturally, obstructed French efforts to rearm, which took place in the face of heavy criticism, from 1934 onwards. Strangely enough, the tanks which trickled haltingly off French production lines were mechanically equal, and in some cases superior, to their German counterparts. The same

7th March 1936. Germany reoccupies the Rhineland – the first major manifestation of the military resurgence of the new Germany

The Munich Pact 1938. Chamberlain and Daladier (centre, left and right) buy time at Czechoslovakia's expense

could not be said of aircraft; here also French production lagged lamentably – in 1939 France made less than 600 first-line aircraft, about one quarter of German production.

Things went from bad to worse. The Popular Front fell in June 1937, and less than a year later Hitler's troops moved into Austria. Daladier, the new premier, joined Neville Chamberlain in buying time at Munich. It soon became obvious, though, that Munich was merely a palliative. Largely due to the efforts of Paul Reynaud, who became Minister of Finance in November 1938, France was jarred into unfamiliar activity. The effort came too late; France had abandoned Czechoslovakia at Munich, and France was denied any hope of Russian assistance by the Russo-German non-aggression pact of 23rd August 1939. Less than a week later the Germans fell on Poland. Britain and France, with an ill-timed concern for the moral obligations they had for so long forgotten, declared war on Germany.

Mobilisation proceeded according to plan, and a French army of sixty-seven divisions, supported by five divisions of the British Expeditionary Force, slid into positions in and around the Maginot Line. In unheard-of boldness, several divisions even lurched forward across the Saar, and reached the outposts of the German Siegfried Line. Meanwhile, Guderian's panzers lacerated Poland, which capitulated after only twenty-eight days. The shock of Poland's defeat persuaded Gamelin to withdraw his forces from the Saar, and to return to the ferro-concrete security of the Maginot Line. The war then settled down to an unspectacular tedium which well merited the title 'phoney war'. The French army vegetated behind its dreary fortifications. Morale and dicipline were not high at the outset, and, as autumn dragged

Paul Reynaud, French Minister of Finance. After Munich he tried to prepare for war, but it was too late

General Georges, C-in-C of the North East Front. His personal antipathy to Gamelin was very divisive

on into winter, both deteriorated. Officers sought staff jobs as a relief from boredom; many ordinary soldiers simply sloped off at the weekend, passes or not. German propaganda contributed to the general air of depression. Particularly successful were German efforts to alienate French and British. Leaflets, showing British troops enjoying themselves in Paris while their French allies endured the freezing misery of the line, were dropped on an audience that was all too receptive.

Ensconced in his headquarters in the grey Château de Vincennes, General Gamelin tugged at the tangled links of the French chain of command. The already disorganised state of the French High Command was not improved by a reorganisation in January 1940; General Doumenc became Chief of Staff, and General Georges Com-mander-in-Chief of the North-East Front. The tangled line of command thus created was further worsened by the mutual antipathy between Gamelin and Georges. Gamelin's strategy, such as it was, was to cover the open northern flank of the Maginot Line by an advance into Belgium, taking up a position on the line of the River Escaut. The fortuitous capture of some secret German documents on 10th January persuaded Gamelin to modify this plan. Instead of an advance into Belgium by some ten divisions, the élite of the French army, together with the majority of the tanks at Gamelin's disposal, was to sweep forward into Belgium to meet the main weight of the German attack.

Unhappily for Gamelin, the brunt of the Wehrmacht's assault was destined to fall elsewhere. The outbreak of war had, ironically, caught the Ger-

21

man General Staff without a plan for offensive operations in the west. The German answer to this lacuna was the plan known as 'Case Yellow'. This envisaged an attack in the north by von Bock's Army Group B, with its centre of gravity in the area of Namur. Further south, Army Groups A and C were given lesser tasks. The plan was pedestrian and uninspiring. Its failings were apparent both to Colonel-General von Rundstedt, commanding Army Group A, and his brilliant Chief of Staff, Erich von Manstein. The latter produced a new, startlingly different plan, designed to bring about what Manstein termed 'a decisive issue by land'. A variety of factors – among them the loss of the secret papers in January – contributed to the eventual adoption of the Manstein plan.

The new formula was as bold as the old one had been cautious. The weight of the attack would be delivered by Army Group A, which was to contain seven panzer divisions. The German armour would rupture the French front between Dinant and Sedan; its advance would be assisted by airborne troops who would seize forts and bridges on the line of advance. The imposing might of the Luftwaffe would ensure German air superiority.

In Paris, meanwhile, the Daladier government fell towards the end of March, and was replaced by a ministry headed by Paul Reynaud. The French army continued to stagnate. By a tragic coincidence, the units holding the sector threatened by Manstein's scheme were of very low quality, even by the unexacting standards of the remainder of the army. General Corap's Ninth Army comprised seven infantry divisions, of which only two were regular; the remaining five contained reservists of doubtful zeal and limited training. General Huntziger's Second Army, also in the path of the German advance, was in little better order. Worse still, the terrain in front of these two armies – the hilly, wooded Ardennes – was regarded as impassable, and its defence entrusted to a cavalry screen.

On the morning of Friday 10th May the Allies were rudely awakened from their torpor. The German offensive burst with unprecedented ferocity. While the Luftwaffe hammered Allied airfields, the mass of German armour poured towards the Ardennes. Parachutists – both real and imagined – sowed confusion behind the lines, and the huge Belgian fortress of Eben-Emael fell to airborne assault. The French First and Seventh Armies, together with the BEF, moved forward into Belgium, while German penetration into the Ardennes deepened. Well ahead of the advance was 7th Panzer Division, soon to be known as the 'Ghost Division', under its brisk, enterprising commander, Major-General Erwin Rommel. The

May 1940. The Phoney War is over. The first German troops enter French territory in the Ardennes

Major-General Erwin Rommel, commander of the 7th Panzer Division, soon known as the 'Ghost Division'

French cavalry screen was roughly handled, and on 12th May the first panzers reached the Meuse at Sedan. Without waiting for the artillery concentration which, in Allied eyes, should have prepared the way for a crossing, the Germans pushed on across the river on the 13th.

Corap's response was all too typical of French efforts to combat the rapidly-deteriorating situation. Counterattacks simply failed to get off the ground; commanders whined about the difficulties confronting them, and the morale of the troops became increasingly ragged. Guderian's crossing of the Meuse on 13th May was covered by a tremendous air bombardment, which could scarcely fail to crack the resolution of Corap's reservists. In the north, the Dutch were clearly at their last gasp, and the Allied forces which had moved into Belgium were experiencing difficulties.

Some units fought well. The *tirailleurs* of General Sancelme's 4th North African Division, consigned by Corap to a defensive rôle which ill suited their temperament, gave a good account of themselves, as did the machine gunners of 42nd Fortress Division, holding the Meuse at Monthermé. The rest of Corap's army went down like driftwood in a torrent. Troops streamed off to the rear, and what little will the French command had ever possessed steadily wilted. With each succeeding day German penetration increased. On 15th May the brittle shell shattered completely, and German armoured columns drove on, down roads encumbered by debris and bewildered streams of prisoners. Overhead, aircraft of the Luftwaffe flickered along the tree-lined roads, machine-gunning refugees and retreating military columns with a cheerful lack of discrimination. Some French armoured units managed to launch local counterattacks, which failed before the concentrated weight of German armour.

On 17th May, Colonel de Gaulle, recently appointed to command the embryo 4th Armoured Division, pressed a counterattack into Montcornet and caused the Germans some anxiety before he was eventually driven off. As the bulge in the French centre deepened, Allied forces fell back from Belgium, chivvied en route by the Luftwaffe. The panzers drove on. St Quentin fell on the morning of 18th May. On the 19th, Gamelin was replaced as C-in-C by General Maxime Weygand. As Weygand took over the reins of command, the weary tank crews of 2nd Panzer Division reached the Atlantic coast, thereby cutting the Allied armies in half. The Germans were, nevertheless, vulnerable; determined Allied counterattacks could still imperil German gains by cutting the panzers off from the infantry divisions to their rear. A British thrust towards Arras on the 21st worried even the unflappable Rommel, but it soon ran out of steam.

Weygand's attempts to dispel the gathering gloom met with little success. The raw material of the 'Weygand Plan' was by now exhausted,

physically and spiritually, hunted by the thrusting German armour and haunted by fear of the 'Fifth Column'. Lord Gort, commander of the BEF, decided, not unwisely, to withdraw his battered forces through the port of Dunkirk – a move hardly calculated to enhance French morale. Weygand's own resolve was weak. On 25th May he admitted to Reynaud that France had 'gone to war with a 1918 army against a German army of 1939. It is sheer madness.'

By 3rd June British evacuation from Dunkirk was complete. Surprisingly, French resolution stiffened. Some of Weygand's 'hedgehogs', groups of infantry and gunners clustered round old 75mm guns, fought with determination. But French belief in victory had gone. On 14th June German troops trundled into a blanched Paris. Two days later Reynaud resigned, and the aged Pétain took over. The latter had already expressed the view that 'An armistice is . . . the necessary condition for the survival of eternal France.' Accordingly, a French delegation met Hitler and his service chiefs in a *wagon-lit* at Réthondes. By a twist of Teutonic irony, it was the same coach in which the Armistice of November 1918 had been signed. Terms were finalised on 22nd June; the wheel had come full circle.

Above : Lord Gort (Commander of the BEF) before the disaster of Dunkirk *Below :* Dunkirk, June 1940. The British abandon France to her fate. *Left :* Hitler accepts France's surrender in the same *wagon-lits* in which Germany had surrendered in November 1918

Free
France

Dunkirk. France had 'gone to war with a 1918 army against a German army of 1939. It is sheer madness', Weygand admitted to Reynaud

During the last tottering days of the Reynaud government, Charles de Gaulle, wearing the newly-acquired star of a Brigadier-General, was sent to London on a liaison mission to the British government. He returned to France on 16th June, but went back to Britain on the following day. At 6 pm on 18th June de Gaulle broadcast a speech over the BBC. He made a scathing attack on the French political and military establishment, but went on to declare that France's defeat was not final. 'France', he declared, 'is not alone. She has behind her a vast Empire. She can join with the British Empire which rules the seas and is continuing the struggle. Like England, she can draw without limit on the immense industrial might of the United States.

'This war is not limited to the unhappy territory of our dear country. The outcome of this war has not been settled by the Battle of France. This is a world war.' He urged all French soldiers or technicians who happened to be in Britain at the time to contact him. 'Whatever happens', stressed de Gaulle, 'the flame of resistance must not go out, and it will not go out.' De Gaulle ignored Weygand's summons to return to France, and in return suggested that Weygand should continue to fight, offering his services to Weygand should he decide to do this. Weygand declined to reply. A military court sitting in France sentenced de Gaulle, in absentia, to a month's imprisonment. This sentence was later changed to one of death.

Unperturbed by his failure with Weygand, de Gaulle proceeded to offer his services to anyone better qualified than he to lead the resistance. On 19th June he telegraphed to General Noguès, C-in-C in North Africa and Resident-General of Morocco, offering to place himself under Noguès' orders if the latter decided to reject the Armistice. Five days later he again wired Noguès, as well as General Mittelhauser, C-in-C in the Levant, M Puaux, High Commissioner of the Levant and General Catroux, Governor-General of Indo-China, suggesting the formation of a defence committee. Eventually, only Catroux rallied to Free France. The remainder of these 'proconsuls' aligned themselves with Pétain's government which soon left its wartime refuge in Bordeaux for the fateful spa of Vichy.

De Gaulle's creation of the Free

French movement faced all Frenchmen with an unpalatable and difficult choice. For the army in particular the decision was particularly painful. Officers and soldiers had to choose between obedience and what was, in effect, rebellion. Even de Gaulle experienced a tremendous wrench in rejecting the orders of an army which he had served all his life. For de Gaulle, the broadcast of 18th June was the turning point. 'As the irrevocable words flew out upon their way', recalled the general, 'I felt within myself a life coming to an end – the life I had lived within the framework of a solid France and individual army. At the age of forty-nine I was entering upon adventure like a man thrown by his fate outside all terms of reference.'

Pétain's Vichy régime possessed qualities which appealed to many Frenchmen. It was right wing, but antimonarchist as well as anticommunist. Stolid and comfortably bureaucratic, it could claim legal continuity from the Third Republic. Pétain, old and garrulous as he was, was undoubtedly sincere. 'The country', he rumbled, 'has been rotted by politicians. The people can no longer discern the face of France through the veil the politicians have thrown over it.' Pétain saw the solution in a return to the salutary basic virtues of *Travaille, Famille, Patrie*. After the upheavals of 1940, most Frenchmen were content to settle for the warm security of Vichy and the charisma of its white-haired leader.

'There is no France without a sword', thundered de Gaulle. Yet his initial efforts to create a weapon for Free France met with only limited success. On 28th June Britain recognised him as leader of the Free French, but gave him little assistance in recruiting such French troops as were in Britain. There were, indeed, several thousand of these men. Several thousand French soldiers had been brought off at Dunkirk, though many of these had already been repatriated. More had been evacuated from Cherbourg and Brest. Many of these men wanted to return home, either to escape into civilian life or to continue serving with Vichy's 100,000-man 'Armistice Army'. Some, however, preferred to rally to Free France. Very few responded to de Gaulle's first appeal on 18th June. Furthermore, the British High Command tended to be unhelpful.

On 29th June de Gaulle visited General Berthouart's Light Mountain Division at Trentham Park. Although the divisional commander himself was anti-German, he considered it his duty as a soldier to return to France. Nevertheless, Bethouart allowed de Gaulle to speak to his men. As a result, much of the 13th Legion Half-Brigade – two battalions – under Lieutenant-Colonel Magrin-Verneret (later known as 'Monclar') rallied to de Gaulle. Acting as Magrin-Verneret's Second-in-Command was a tall, thin-faced captain of Alsatian stock, Marie-Pierre Koenig; he too threw in his lot with Free France. Despite the fact that the troops were warned by the British that their action would be regarded by Vichy as rebellion, several *Chasseurs Alpins*, most of a tank company, and some artillerymen and engineers, followed suit. On the next

General Berthouart, commander of the Light Mountain Division which had escaped to Britain

day de Gaulle tried to visit the camps at Aintree and Haydock, but British authorities, fearing that such a move might be prejudicial to order, refused to allow him to do so.

De Gaulle's efforts at recruiting were further impeded by the events of 3rd July. A British squadron attacked French warships at Mers-el-Kébir, near Oran, killing over 1,000 French sailors, in an effort to prevent the French fleet falling into German hands. Some French naval units, albeit small ones, did succeed in escaping to Britain, both before and after the tragedy of Mers-el-Kébir. The submarines *Rubis* and *Narval*, together with several light surface craft, put into British ports. All the able-bodied men from the island of Sein arrived at Cornwall in fishing boats. Men trickled in from various sources, and by the end of July de Gaulle had about 7,000 men at his disposal, in varying states of disarray, carrying a bewildering variety of arms. It was, nevertheless, a start.

One of de Gaulle's most urgent needs was to place his dealings with the British government on a securely-established footing. On 23rd June the

British government declared that the Bordeaux government could not be considered independent, and expressed its intention of recognising the French National Committee, set up by de Gaulle. On the 28th de Gaulle was recognised as leader of the Free French, but it was not until August that an agreement between the general and the British government was finalised. General de Gaulle was recognised as 'supreme commander' of Free French forces, which would, however, operate under 'the general directives of the British High Command'. British financial aid to the Free French would, insisted de Gaulle, be repaid at the end of the war. There was to be 'permanent liaison' between British and French, to decide upon the use to be made of Free French merchant ships and their crews. Free French HQ was set up in Carlton Gardens, and here de Gaulle installed his team.

Disappointingly few great names had joined him. Nonetheless, he was able to establish a workable organisation which contained several very able men. Professor René Cassin acted as the general's assistant, and the capable René Pleven handled what de Gaulle termed 'our minute finances'. Maurice Schumann was the principal Free French speaker in the ten minutes of radio time that the BBC allowed de Gaulle each day. Massip dealt with the Press, and Bingen with Free French shipping.

The nascent Free French navy was commanded by that enigmatic figure, Admiral Muselier, who was ably assisted by Captain Thierry d'Argenlieu. On land, Magrin-Verneret commanded Free French forces, supported by Koenig. The small but bellicose Free French airforce was under the command of Major Pijeaud. The general's staff comprised Hettier de Boislambert, Dewrin and Tissier. De Gaulle's young aide-de-camp, Lieu-

Captain Marie-Pierre Koenig, one of de Gaulle's earliest recruits

tenant Geoffrey de Courcel, acted as the general's *chef de cabinet* and interpreter. Liaison with the British was conducted through General Sir Edward Spears, who had held a similar liaison post in the First World War. His 'tenacity and dexterity', wrote de Gaulle, 'were at these harsh early stages more than valuable – essential.' A serious problem was inherent in the composition of de Gaulle's inner circle. Many of the general's advisers were men of the Right, and had avowed political ambitions. This naturally tended to discredit de Gaulle in certain circles. It must also be remembered that de Gaulle was not particularly well known; his military career had, so far, not been conspicuously successful. There were those who saw de Gaulle as motivated primarily by self-interest. The general was undoubtedly austere and autocratic, but his attempts to find someone better qualified than himself to lead Free France were certainly sincere, and should, to a great degree, refute charges of self-seeking. Nevertheless, even in London there existed several groups who were extremely vocal in their opposition to de Gaulle.

One of de Gaulle's primary considerations was the acquisition of a territorial base, independent of British control. Africa seemed the most attractive location for such a base. 'In the vast spaces of Africa', wrote de Gaulle, 'France could in fact recreate for herself an army and a sovereignty.' Prospects in North Africa seemed poor. The terms of the Armistice left French colonies in North Africa free from German occupation. Aspects of Vichy's 'National Revolution' were not without appeal, particularly to men of substance and members of the administration. The first glimmer of hope came from central Africa. Felix Eboué, Governor of Chad, collaborated with the local military commander, Colonel Marchand, and on 26th August declared the colony Free French. On the following day Colonel Leclerc engineered a similar coup in Douala, capital of the French Cameroons. Brazzaville, capital of French Equatorial Africa, fell to troops from Chad, led by Colonel de Larminat.

These dramatic events gave de Gaulle control of a large part of central Africa, and encouraged him to continue with territorial acquisition in that continent. One of the results of this was the inglorious Dakar affair. The great naval base of Dakar was of dual significance. It was strategically situated within easy striking distance of the Atlantic shipping lanes, and hence would be of great value to the Germans. Secondly, the seizure of Dakar by de Gaulle would be of tremendous political significance. On 23rd September an Anglo-French squadron appeared off Dakar, but its presence failed to shake the resolution of Governor-General Baisson, who was determined to adhere to Vichy. Shots were exchanged. Dakar was bombarded on the next day, and both sides suffered telling losses. On the 26th the British and Free French ships slipped away, leaving Dakar firmly in Vichy hands. The Dakar fiasco was a severe blow to Free French morale, and a useful propaganda victory for Vichy. Nevertheless, in the main, the African situation continued to improve. De Gaulle visited the Cameroons on 8th October, and moved on to Chad. At Fort Lamy, capital of that colony, he met General Catroux, formerly Governor-General of Indo-China. Catroux was very much senior to de Gaulle in terms of military rank, but he at once offered to serve under de Gaulle, recognising that the latter's position was outside the normal hierarchy. From Chad, de Gaulle went to Brazzaville, where, on 27th October, he set up the *Conseil de Défence de l'Empire*. This was to consist of de Gaulle and eight other members, including General Catroux, Admiral Muselier, Professor Cassin, General de Larminat and Colonel Leclerc.

32

While the *Conseil de Défence* came into being, operations were undertaken against Gabon, one of the remaining Vichyite colonies in Africa. A force under Leclerc left Douala for Libreville by sea; the land forces, a colonial battalion and a battalion of the Foreign Legion, were led by Koenig. Libreville was taken after a brief action, and the pro-Vichy Governor, Masson, subsequently committed suicide. Although the colonies of Upper Volta and Niger remained in Vichy hands, de Gaulle now had, in central Africa, the territorial base he sought. He returned to London on 17th November, and arrived in a Britain gloomy with the blackout and pounded by German bombs.

Morale in Britain was uncertain. The Battle of Britain had, it is true been won, but the submarine war continued to rage. Shipping was a constant preoccupation, and losses mounted alarmingly. The Mediterranean was unsafe, and the great majority of convoys were condemned to the long voyage around the Cape. Relations with America remained uncertain. America showed no signs of entering the war, and 'Lend-Lease' was not as yet in force. Convoys to and from America ran the gauntlet of prowling U-boats in the North Atlantic. The international situation looked black, and within Britain herself there were few encouraging signs. Determination to resist remained steadfast, but the material at hand for such resistance was all too scarce. Small wonder, then, that Churchill did not look upon the activities of the Free French with enthusiasm.

There were some minor causes for elation. In the Western Desert, a French battalion performed sterling service in General O'Connor's offensive against the Italians, and Leclerc's troops took the Italian-held oasis of Al Kufrah in southern Libya. For the Free French, these gains were overshadowed by the Muselier affair. The admiral was arrested by the British on charges of treason which

Generals Catroux (above) and Leclerc (below). Catroux, the Governor-General of Indo-China, rallied to de Gaulle shortly after Dunkirk, while Leclerc (then a Colonel) engineered a Free French *coup* in the Cameroons two months later

were, it later transpired, based on documents forged by Vichy agents. One of the immediate results of the affair was the 'jurisdiction' agreement of 15th January 1941, which permitted the Free French to set up their own military courts in Britain. The incident had, however, strained relations between de Gaulle and the British, and helped worsen the general's personal relations with Muselier. In March the financial negotiations between them were successfully concluded. A system of central payment was devised, and a rate of exchange agreed upon.

There remained the question of Metropolitan France. The Resistance movement was as yet undeveloped, and totally without control or coordination. De Gaulle decided to branch out into what he termed 'clandestine action'. The Free French commenced the underground war with numerous disadvantages. The main source of potential opposition to the Germans within France lay in the 100,000-man 'Armistice Army', in the southern, unoccupied, zone. Certain elements within the Vichy army succeeded in concealing large quantities of arms and equipment, and preparing a clandestine mobilisation plan. But de Gaulle's contact with the Vichy army was negligible; many of its officers and soldiers had deliberately chosen Vichy rather than Free France, and could therefore not be expected to cooperate with the general. There was nothing within de Gaulle's organisation which suggested that it might have any aptitude for Intelligence or espionage; volunteers for such work abounded, but they lacked training. Fortunately for de Gaulle, several of his adherents showed considerable flair for Intelligence. Major Dewawrin, soon known as 'Colonel Passy', showed remarkable ability in setting up and running the *Bureau Central de Renseignements et d'Action* (BCRA), the Free French Intelligence organisation.

The question of action within

Left: December 1940. Free French patrol in the Bardia area, Western Desert. *Above:* General O'Connor, British Commander, Western Desert

France proved yet another fruitful source of conflict with the British. Special Operations Executive (SOE) had been set up in mid-July 1940; its task, as broadly defined by Churchill, was 'to set Europe ablaze'. But while one section of SOE worked in cooperation with BCRA, another operated quite independently of, and sometimes at variance with, de Gaulle's men. The political situation within France had deteriorated since the signing of the Armistice. In early July 1940 a Constitutional Act had replaced the Third Republic by a new 'Etat Français', with the regal figure of 'We, Philippe Pétain, Marshal of France', at its head. Under Pétain, the government was in the hands of Pierre Laval, soon to be temporarily replaced by Admiral Darlan. The latter seemed alarmingly collaborationist. On 11th May he visited Hitler at the German leader's mountain retreat of Berchtesgaden, and concluded an agreement which was intended to ensure Vichy military

cooperation against the British in the Middle East. This agreement was to have the deplorable effect of setting the supporters of Vichy and Free France at each other's throats.

As early as 14th July 1940, de Gaulle had contacted General Wavell, British C-in-C in the Middle East, asking him to form units of the Free French elements in his area, and send them as reinforcements to General Legentilhomme in Djibouti. It was just as well that Wavell did not comply with de Gaulle's request, for it soon became apparent that Djibouti had no intention of rallying to Free France. A marine infantry battalion, which happened to be in Cyprus when the Armistice was signed, joined the Free French and distinguished itself at Sidi Barrani, in the Western Desert.

On 11th and 18th December de Gaulle ordered de Larminat and Catroux to send a force from French Equatorial Africa to the Middle East. This force was to consist of a Legion half-brigade, a Senegalese battalion from

35

Chad, a company of marines, a squadron of tanks, together with supporting services. Colonel Monclar was in command. French troops were already in action alongside the British against the Italians in Eritrea. Major Jourdier had brought over some-*Spahis* from Syria in June 1940, and some airmen had flown to Egypt from Syria and Tunis. The Senegalese battalion of Monclar's force travelled to Eritrea in largely commandeered lorries along the appalling tracks from Khartoum, and went into action near Kub Kub on 20th February. De Gaulle's *Memoirs* note his vexation at the fact that French troops at Djibouti adhered to Vichy, even though their commander, General Legentilhomme, went over to the Free French. Nevertheless, Monclar's troops did well in Eritrea, fighting with dash and courage beside the British at Keren. Monclar himself had the unusual honour of receiving the surrender of the commander of the Italian Red Sea Fleet. Free French troops took nearly 15,000 prisoners during the course of the victorious campaign.

Leclerc, meanwhile, had been operating in the desert, against Italian forces in the Al Kufrah area. The oasis itself fell on 1st March, and de Gaulle at once ordered de Larminat to prepare for the reconquest of the Fezzan. This operation had to be cancelled owing to the changing military situation in Libya. In March 1941 de Gaulle himself visited the Middle East. 'A vital game was being played there', he wrote. 'We therefore had to be in it . . . everything required us to be present at the battles of which the canal was the stake.' The Suez canal was indeed at stake. The newly arrived German forces lunged into the attack in April, and British troops were driven out of Libya and Cyrenaica. In the same month German forces poured into Greece in overwhelming strength. Anglo-Greek resistance collapsed on 24th April. The military problems facing Wavell were serious enough,

and he was further troubled by political interference. His army contained numerous Dominion contingents, from Austria, New Zealand and South Africa, whose governments cast a watchful eye over the handling of their troops. In addition, Churchill was in constant contact with Wavell, offering advice and suggestions that were not entirely welcome.

A further cross for the harrassed Wavell to bear was the restless situation in the Arab countries. There was the disturbing possibility that the Germans might use the Vichy French airfields in Syria as bases for air attacks on the Suez canal. Such a use of French airfields had been sanctioned by the Berchtesgaden meeting of 11th May. There was, furthermore, no reason why German activity in Syria should be confined to aircraft. If German ground forces were to be concentrated in Syria the canal would be dangerously vulnerable. In Iraq, too, the situation was ominous; Rashid Ali was fermenting discontent against the British.

The reaction of the 30,000 French troops in Syria was, obviously, of prime importance. Their commander, General Dentz, was described by de Gaulle as 'an extremely conventional General Officer who was ready to apply strictly the orders given him by Darlan.' Free French propaganda had little effect upon the troops in Syria. De Gaulle and Catroux soon realised that costly military operations against Syria could be averted only if Dentz were to be attacked by very strong British and Free French forces. The British were less sure; Wavell in particular did not look forward to the opening of a new front. The British government was anxious to win over Dentz by peaceful means if this was at all possible. To this end, a commercial treaty was concluded at the end of April, ensuring food supply to Syria and the Leb-

French Spahis, brought to the Western Desert from Syria in August 1940

anon. On 9th May de Gaulle was advised by Spears that no attack on Syria was contemplated for the moment; Spears further advised de Gaulle against going to Egypt. Shortly after this meeting, the situation in the Levant became critical. The Iraqis, prompted by Rashid Ali, rose against the British, who were literally besieged on their airfields. On 12th May German aircraft arrived in Syria, and Dentz received orders from Vichy to cooperate fully with the Germans. Two days later the British reversed their earlier decision, and determined to invade Syria.

It was depressingly apparent that Dentz would not give up without a struggle. He had over 30,000 men at his disposal, well-provided with artillery, tanks and aircraft. In addition, there were numerous locally-raised Syrian and Lebanese troops available. To oppose this powerful force, the Free French under Legentilhomme had only 6,000 infantry, with eight guns, ten tanks and twenty-four planes. Free French Intelligence services had, however, discovered that if a massive attack was launched from several directions, Dentz's resistance would only be token. It was therefore imperative

that the Free French thrust should be heavily supported by the British. Wavell, harried by Churchill's telegrams and preoccupied by the military situation in Libya, was naturally disinclined to hazard strong forces in the Syrian venture.

Early on the morning of 8th June 1941 Anglo-French forces invaded Syria. One Australian infantry brigade moved down the coast road, and another made for Merjayan. To the east, Legentilhomme's Free French Division, supported by Brigadier Lloyd's 5th Indian Infantry Brigade, crossed the frontier near Der'ā. General Wilson, in Cairo, was in overall command of the invasion; the Australian General Laverack controlled actual operations from his HQ at Nazareth. De Gaulle had visited some of Legentilhomme's men on 26th May, and considered them to be of like mind to himself; bitter at being forced to fight against Frenchmen, but nonetheless determined to invade. Other sources are less wholehearted in their descriptions of Free French morale. It must, though, be

Free French and British forces invade Syria in June 1940, and are bitterly resisted by Vichy French troops

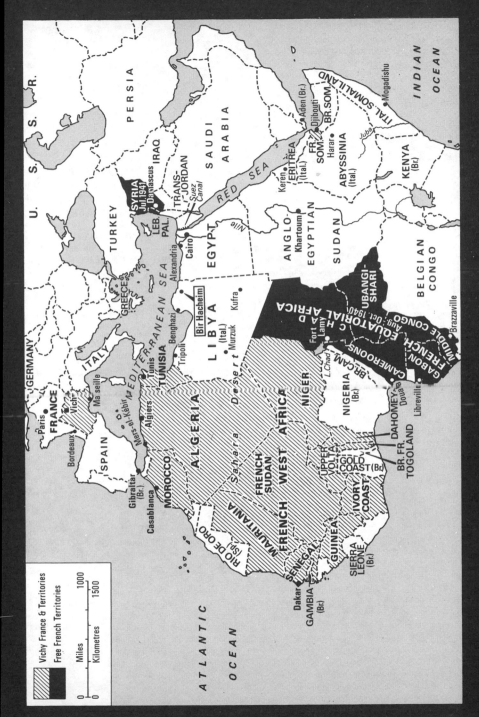

Vichy and Free French territories in North Africa

A French armoured car, Syria. On 12th July 1941 Dentz's Vichy French force requested an Armistice. De Gaulle was infuriated when Syria and Lebanon were placed under British rule and the Vichy troops were repatriated

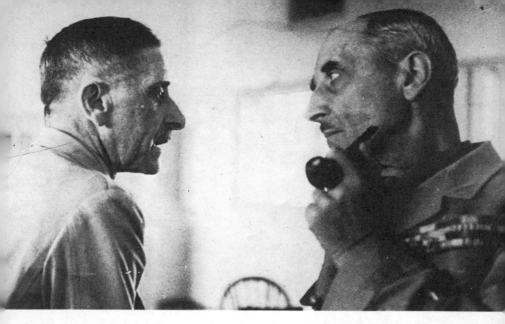

admitted that Legentilhomme faced a heartrending task.

The fighting in Syria was bitter and confused. Legentilhomme's division moved steadily north, meeting with stiff resistance. Koenig, now a Lieutenant-Colonel, was serving as Legentilhomme's GSO 1, lending his phlegmatic aura to divisional HQ. By an irony sadly typical of the invasion, Legentilhomme's adversary, General de Verdilhac, commanding the Vichy troops defending Damascus, had been at St-Cyr and Staff College with Legentilhomme. The two men knew each other well, and Legentilhomme strove to anticipate the future actions of his friend and opponent. Casualties on both sides were heavy. The British and Free French lost over 4,000 killed and wounded. Among the killed was one of the Free French brigade commanders; Legentilhomme himself was wounded. Dentz's forces incurred over 6,000 casualties. With the crushing of Rashid Ali's rebellion in Iraq, the British were able to reinforce their forces in Syria; Dentz requested an Armistice on 12th July. De Gaulle was later to imply that the relatively small numbers of British troops

Generals de Verdillac (Vichy) and Catroux (Free French) talk amicably after the Armistice in Syria

initially employed accounted for the strength of Vichy resistance. It should, though, be appreciated that the British were short of troops in the Middle East, while Syria, as one of a number of fronts, lacked the significance for the British that it obviously possessed for the French.

The conclusion of peace terms was to strain relations between British and Free French almost to breaking point. De Gaulle had outlined to Churchill terms which would be acceptable to Free France, but was gravely disappointed with the St Jean d'Acre agreement, whose terms seemed in direct opposition to Free French interests. Vichy forces were to be repatriated, complete with their equipment, to France. No opportunity was to be given for de Gaulle to win them over. Syrian and Lebanese troops were to be placed directly under British command; Syria and Lebanon were themselves to be transferred to British rule.

De Gaulle was infuriated. He regarded the agreement as an astonishing piece of chicanery designed to increase British influence in the Arab world. His response was swift and unequivocal. He instantly repudiated the agreement, and on 21st July met Oliver Lyttleton, Minister of State in the British government, in Cairo, and repeated his denunciation. De Gaulle informed Lyttleton that in three days time Free French forces would no longer be under British command. Catroux, furthermore, had been instructed to assume authority in Syria and the Lebanon, resisting opposition from any quarter – including the British. De Gaulle then sent a telegram informing Churchill of these facts.

British efforts at conciliation resulted, on 25th July, in acceptance of French rights in Syria and the Lebanon. The Free French were allowed to contact Dentz's soldiers with a view to recruiting them. But of the French troops in the Levant, only 127 officers and 6,000 NCOs and men went over to de Gaulle. The Free French had a greater degree of success with the locally-raised troops; 290 officers and 14,000 NCOs and men from these units rallied to de Gaulle. De Gaulle maintained that the paucity of French troops who came over to Free France was directly due to British refusal to let him recruit earlier. This is very much open to question. It would be too much to expect troops who had fought hard and well to desert to their opponents on the conclusion of peace, exchanging life in the firmly-established Vichy army for what could only be a hazardous career with the Free French. The Syrian affair, which dragged on for some months after the cessation of hostilities there, had important political ramifications. It brought relations between de Gaulle and the British to the verge of collapse, and was responsible for new Anglo-French friction in the Middle East

One of the indirect results of Operation Barbarossa, the German invasion of Russia, was Moscow's recognition, on 26th September 1941, of de Gaulle

as leader of the Free French. General Petit was dispatched on a liaison mission to Russia, and in January 1942 de Gaulle met Molotov in London. De Gaulle was profoundly moved by the gigantic struggle in the Soviet Union. He appreciated that Russia was the most important theatre of war; without German preoccupation with the east, the Allies had little chance of victory elsewhere. There was a powerful temptation for de Gaulle to break away from the British altogether, and to join instead with the Soviet Union. When de Gaulle's representatives, Cassin and Dejean, visited Maisky, the Soviet Ambassador in London, on 8th August 1941, they emphasised that de Gaulle had 80,000 men under arms. They were, perhaps, less eager to point out that this total included a large number of colonial troops, Africans, Syrians and Lebanese, and that all Free French units were far from fully-equipped. In November, the possibility of the employment of French troops in Russia was brought up. At the time, the British were refusing to employ Larminat's Free French Division in the Western Desert; no secret was made of de Gaulle's overtures to Russia, indicating that the French offer was intended, in part at least, to put pressure on the British.

As the military strength and political influence of Free France grew, de Gaulle felt the need for a more formalised administration. Accordingly, on 24th September the National Committee was instituted. This committee had all the characteristics of a provisional government. It consisted of various *commissaires*, each responsible for a particular department. De Gaulle was head of the committee, and the *commissaires* included Pleven, with responsibility for the economy, finances and the colonies, Cassin, dealing with justice and public administration, and Dejead, in charge of foreign affairs. General Legentilhomme was *commissaire* for war, and Diethelm supervised action in Metro-

Admiral Muselier, naval chief in de Gaulle's 'Provisional Government'

Admiral Thierry d'Argenlieu, member without portfolio

politan France, labour and information. Admiral Muselier was in charge of naval affairs, and Catroux and Thierry d'Argenlieu were members without portfolio. Affairs were discussed collectively. The committee functioned well until the second of the Muselier crises, in March 1942. The admiral resigned from the committee on 3rd March; de Gaulle placed him on the reserve, and replaced him by Admiral Auboyneau. Muselier refused to hand over command of the Free French fleet, and received a degree of backing from the British Admiralty. Unfortunately for Muselier, he did not receive the same support from the officers of the Free French navy, who stood by de Gaulle and Auboyneau. Muselier thus had no choice but to go into retirement.

Before his untimely departure from the scene, Muselier had been instrumental in bringing about the seizure of the islands of St-Pierre and Miquelon. America's entry into the war, following the Japanese attack on Pearl Harbor on 7th December, had not produced the immediate *rapprochement* between Free France and America for which de Gaulle had hoped. Several French ships – including the liner *Normandie* – which happened to be in American ports at the time of America's entry into the war were requisitioned without so much as a by-your-leave. The Declaration of the United Nations was signed, later that month, by twenty-six governments; Free France was not asked to participate. The islands of St-Pierre and Miquelon lie off the coast of Newfoundland. They were, in December 1941, under Vichy administration, and, although the British were in favour of bringing them over to de Gaulle, the Americans were in process of concluding an agreement with the Vichy representative whereby the islands would become neutral. Muselier, acting on de Gaulle's instructions, moved in on 24th December, and found the populace very much in favour of Free France. The Americans were furious, but were obliged to accept the *fait accompli*.

Cooperation between Free France and America was decidedly better in the Pacific. With the rapidly-worsening situation in that theatre, French possessions – New Caledonia, the Marquesas and the Society Islands, among others – became extremely important. The National Committee agreed to allow the Americans whatever they demanded with regard to French Pacific possessions, on the condition that the Americans recognised and respected French authority in these areas. Even before Pearl Harbor, the situation in the Pacific colonies had been far from ideal. The best of the local troops had been mobilised and sent to the Middle East, forming Lieutenant-Colonel Broché's *Bataillon du Pacifique*. Brunot, formerly Governor-General of the Cameroons, was sent to the Pacific on a tour of inspection, and elicited howls of protest by his high-handed methods. To stabilise things, de Gaulle sent Captain (later Admiral) Thierry d'Argenlieu to the Pacific as High Commissioner in July 1941. D'Argenlieu, a capable and diplomatic individual, succeeded in putting affairs on a firm footing by the time of Japanese entry into the war.

The disasters which followed Pearl Harbor had the effect of producing

excellent cooperation between the Free French and the Americans, for a time at least. French reinforcements were sent to the Pacific – with the regrettable loss of the giant submarine *Surcouf,* which went down with all hands following a collision. The Americans undertook to respect French sovereignty. D'Argenlieu liased effectively with General Patch, commanding American land forces in the Pacific. Some friction soon arose between d'Argenlieu and Patch, but this was rapidly submerged in the face of the Japanese threat. In the event, the majority of French possessions in the Pacific remained safe; the Japanese were thwarted in the Coral Sea, and did not succeed in mounting an attack against New Caledonia.

Despite his frequent visits to Africa and the Middle East, de Gaulle himself remained based in London. He initially lived in the Connaught Hotel, with a country house first in Shropshire and later at Berkhamstead. He finally moved to Hampstead. The general was accompanied by his wife and family. His daughter Anne

The giant French submarine *Surcouf* which went down with all hands

Left: General and Madame de Gaulle, **Above:** November 1941. His power and prestige growing, de Gaulle holds a 'manifestation of National Unity' at the Albert Hall

was a boarder with the Dames de Sion, and his son Philippe passed through the *Ecole Navale* and served as a naval officer. De Gaulle spent much of his time in his office at Carlton Gardens, dealing with correspondence and receiving reports. He made frequent visits to British ministers, staff conferences and the like. The general also visited the various centres of French activity in London, such as Professor Saurat's *Institut Français*, the French Chamber of Commerce, and the French hospital.

Less than two months after the formation of the National Committee, de Gaulle made a public statement of policy. On 15th November 1941 he addressed a packed Albert Hall, and affirmed Free French intentions and aspirations. 'Article One', asserted the general, 'is to wage war; that is to say, to give the French effort in the conflict the greatest possible extent and power . . . Article Two is to restore the people to power . . .' Article Three outlined the qualities with which the Free French sought to endow a liberated France; these qualities were, maintained de Gaulle, epitomised by the phrases 'Honour and Country' and 'Liberty, Equality and Fraternity', The general's speech was received with tremendous enthusiasm, by both the crowd in the Albert Hall and the much wider audience to whom the speech was subsequently broadcast.

Although Free French military forces as a whole were based on Brazzaville, a good deal of training was carried out in Britain. At Camberley in Surrey, Colonel Renouard commanded a training unit consisting of a battalion of *chasseurs*, an artillery battery- and a squadron of tanks. NCOs and specialists emerged from this unit every six months. There was also an artillery park, commanded by Major Boutet, whose men were concerned in reconditioning French equipment which had been brought over to Britain in 1940. A good deal of material was provided in this way, and many of de Gaulle's troops were able to use the Lebel rifles and 75mm field guns with which they were already familiar. Some of the 75's dated from the First World War, but were modified by the substitution of rubber-tyred wheels for the older, steel-rimmed, type. Some of this work was carried out at Boutet's artillery park, and, after the invasion of Syria, by the artillery workshops in Beirut. Some equipment was provided by the British and Americans, the former in pursuance of the agreement of 7th August 1940, and the latter under the terms of 'Lend-Lease'. The *Service d'Armement*, initially under Colonel Morin, and later under Major Hirsh, was responsible for negotiations and decisions regarding such equipment.

If Free French land forces were to some extent dependent upon Allied logistic support, the Free French navy was almost exclusively so. This navy remained, as de Gaulle put it, 'purely

national'; it vessels flew the tricolour, and its crews wore French uniform and acknowledged French discipline. Nevertheless, the maintenance and resupply of the vessels was in the hands of the British, who also exercised overall operational command of Free French warships. By June 1942 there were 3,000 Free French sailors, together with a battalion of *fusiliers-marins*. Several Free French ships had already been lost, and over 700 sailors had perished. There were over thirty Free French warships in service at this time, some of which were of French origin, while others had been provided by the British. The Free French fleet was bedevilled by a shortage of officers. To combat this deficiency, a naval cadet school was set up. Another fruitful source of officers was the French merchant navy, many of whose officers held reserve commissions. The Free French merchant navy was

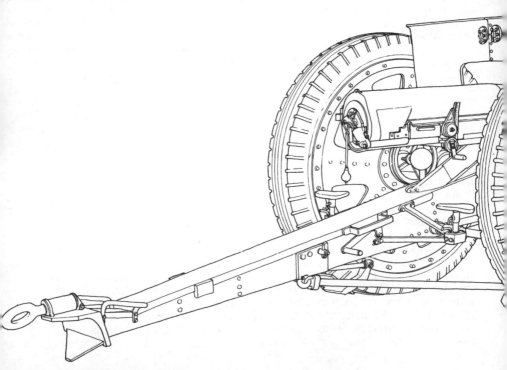

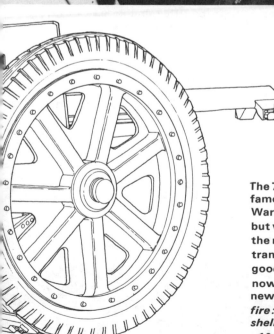

The 75mm field gun, France's most famous artillery piece of the First World War, was still in service in the Second, but with a new carriage more suited to the more sophisticated mechnical transport of the times. Though still a good and reliable weapon, it had by now been completely outclassed by newer guns. *Weight:* 2,700lbs. *Rate of fire:* 6 rounds per minute. *Weight of shell:* 16lbs (shrapnel). *Elevation:* −10 degrees to +19 degrees. *Range:* 7,500 yards remarkably active in its own right. One hundred and seventy merchant vessels had come over to Free France, and all-French crews manned sixty-seven of these, twenty of which were lost during the course of the war. Merchant sailors suffered heavily; of the 580 officers and 4,300 seamen manning these ships, about one quarter had died by mid-1942.

The Free French air force had come into being only after considerable debate. The British, quite understandably, were eager to incorporate French pilots into the Royal Air Force. De Gaulle refused to agree to this. By early 1941 there existed some extemporised French squadrons, while several French airmen were loosely attached to British units. Early in 1941 de Gaulle concluded an agreement with Air-Marshal Longmore in the Middle East, whereby the French were to operate two fighter and two bomber squadrons. In London, Colonel Valin negotiated with Sir Archibald Sinclair, the British Air Minister, and produced, by April 1941, an agreement upon which the Free French air force was founded. By the terms of this agreement, French pilots would be combined, wherever possible, into French squadrons, with equipment and administrative backing supplied by the British. Pilots for whom there was no room in French units were to serve with the RAF, but in the capacity of attached French officers, wearing French uniforms. Three French officers rose to command RAF squadrons; two of them were killed. The toll of dead among French aircrew was high, amounting to twice as many as the effective strength of the Free French air arm at any one time.

Throughout 1941, Free French military strength steadily increased on land, at sea, and in the air. The Syrian affair, tragic though it was, showed that Free French troops were prepared to fight. 1941 saw the detailed formulation of Free French policy, and witnessed close, albeit erratic, cooperation between de Gaulle and the British. The uncertain relations between Free France and America, though imperilled by the seizure of St-Pierre and Miquelon, were strengthened by the Japanese meance. The Soviet Union's entry into the war gave de Gaulle renewed confidence in victory, and, indeed, the chance of an alternative sponsor. Despite the general's interest in Russia, though, there can be little doubt that as 1941 drew to a close, his eyes turned towards the desert battlefields of North Africa.

By the end of 1941 Free French strength on land, in the air and at sea had increased greatly, and de Gaulle considered action in North Africa

The desert war

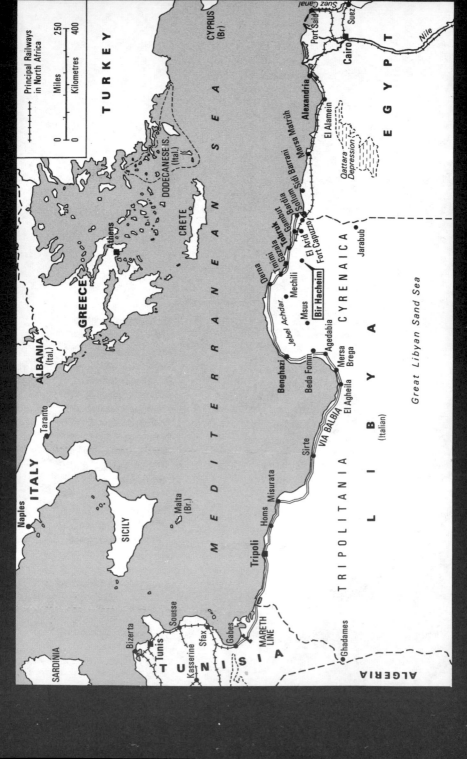

General von Ravenstein – characterised the desert as 'the tactician's paradise and the quartermaster's nightmare'

Rommel in North Africa – 'It was only in the desert that the principles of armoured warfare could be fully applied'

It is the fate of many worthwhile men to be remembered largely because of a chance comment which has become a well-used epigram. General von Ravenstein, a capable German divisional commander, has left only a small mark upon military history. He did, however, succeed in summing up the desert in one crisp phrase – 'The tactician's paradise and the quartermaster's nightmare.' Ravenstein's commander in the desert, Erwin Rommel, enlarged upon the tactical significance of the desert war. 'It was only in the desert', he wrote, 'that the principles of armoured warfare as they were taught in theory before the war could be fully applied and thoroughly developed. It was only in the desert that real tank battles were fought by large-scale formations.'

The Western Desert stretches in a sandy sprawl for over 500 miles, from the Nile to the uplands of Tripolitania. The terrain is uncompromising and the climate harsh. The desert consists of broad plains, divided by a series of ridges, running, in the main, east-west. The width of the desert, from north to south, varies sharply. In the east, near El Alamein, there is a mere forty miles of desert between the sea and the almost impassable Qattâra Depression. From here, the desert broadens as it moves westwards, and for most of Cyrenaica it is almost 200 miles in depth, bordered by the Mediterranean to the north and the Great Libyan Sand Sea to the south.

Vegetation is sparse. Patches of thorny scrub scatter the surface of the desert. The soil itself is an arid mixture of sand and rock. One of the most notable things about the desert,

Left: German transports in the mud
near Cyrenaica. *Above:* Three months
after declaring war, Bersaglieri
motorcyclists lead Graziani's
invasion of Egypt, September 1940

from the military point of view, is the
almost complete lack of water. There
are some springs near the coast, and
a few wells ringed by palm trees in
the interior. For centuries the inhabitants of this region have attemp-
ted to trap the meagre rainfall in
large stone cisterns, known as *Birs*.
Over the years, these have become
disused or damaged, but often their
jagged outlines, half-covered by drift-
ing sand, remain as landmarks on the
bleak surface of the desert.

The climate combines extremes of
temperature. The blistering heat of
daytime gives way, at night, to a
chilling cold. A further unpleasant

complication are sandstorms, in which
gale-force winds drive swirling sand
across the desert. The effects of
desert terrain and climate upon both
men and vehicles may well be imagined. Troops had to fight and live under
conditions of unyielding severity.
Vehicles became stuck in the sand, or
had their engines choked by its wind-
driven particles. Supply was a constant problem; petrol, ammunition,
food and water had to be brought
great distances across ground which
taxed the most skillful navigators
and the most robust vehicles.

Italy had entered the war on 18th
June 1940 in an effort to capitalise
upon the collapse of France. For
Italy, Africa offered interesting military possibilities. Mussolini already
had a foothold in the continent, a
foothold which could be usefully
expanded at British expense. His

propaganda had long proclaimed the Mediterranean to be *'Mare Nostrum'*; the onset of war would give the Italian navy a chance to turn this boast into reality. British possessions in the Middle East were perilously vulnerable; Wavell had just under 90,000 troops with which to hold Egypt, Palestine, and British territory in North-East Africa. The Suez canal was an attractive strategic target; later, after Hitler's attack on Russia, the oilfields of the Caspian offered another, if more distant, goal.

Mussolini's offensive against the British opened successfully. In early August 1940 Italian troops invaded Somaliland, and, in the following month, Marshal Graziani's army of 250,000 men began its advance into Egypt. Graziani reached Sidi Barrani, well inside the Egyptian frontier, halted irresolutely, and set about constructing a series of defensive positions. Wavell prepared to exploit Graziani's over-caution.

The British counteroffensive was to be carried out by the 31,000-strong Western Desert Force, commanded by Major-General R N O'Connor. O'Connor's attack was well-planned, and was carried out with commendable skill and initiative. Early on the

British losses in the counterattack against the Italians, December 1940

morning of 9th December 1940 the Western Desert Force struck at the Italian defences at Nibciwa, Sofafi and Tummar. These positions were swiftly over-run; Sidi Barrani fell next day. O'Connor's troops pushed on along the coast, taking the fortified towns of Bardia and Tobruk. At Tmimi, near the eastern end of the Jebel Achdar – the 'Green Mountains' of Cyrenaica – O'Connor sent some elements of his force cross-

Above: 10th December. Matilda tanks drive the Italians out of Egypt
Below: By February Wavell and O'Connor had captured 130,000 prisoners

British infantry, no longer on the advance, find cover for sniping

country, by way of Mechili and Msus, to cut the coast road at Beda Fomm This cut-off detachment reached the coast road on 5th February, and captured a large Italian convoy that evening. On the 6th, the main Italian force appeared, moving down the coast road, with O'Connor in hot pursuit. There was a brisk action, in the course of which the Italians lost eighty-four tanks. General Bergenzoli, who had replaced Graziani, surrendered next day. The campaign had been strikingly successful. Ten Italian divisions had been destroyed; the Western Desert Force had taken 130,000 prisoners, 380 tanks and 845 guns, for the loss of less than 2,000 killed, wounded and missing.

At sea, too, things went badly for Mussolini. At Taranto on 11th November, Swordfish torpedo-bombers from HMS *Illustrious* disposed of three Italian battleships, and several other warships. Just over four months later, on 27th March 1941, Italian seapower suffered a further blow. An Italian squadron encountered Ad-miral Cunningham's battle fleet off Cape Matapan and was roughly handled, loosing three *Zara* class cruisers, as well as two destroyers.

Fortune also favoured British arms in East Africa. Wavell's troops had been evacuated from British Somaliland by sea following the successful Italian advance of August 1940. The territory was not, however, destined to remain in Italian hands for long. At a conference in Cairo on 2nd December, Wavell outlined his plans for a counteroffensive. Lieutenant-General Sir William Platt was to advance into Eritrea from the Sudan, while Lieutenant-General Sir Alan Cunningham moved north from Kenya into Italian Somaliland. Both prongs of this far-flung pincer movement made good progress, despite the resistance of the Duke of Aosta's 350,000 Italians. Platt pushed into Eritrea, beat General Frusci at Agordat, and battered at Keren, key to the main Kassala-Asmara road. After a resolute defence, Keren fell on 27th March. Asmara was taken six days later, and the port of Massawa on 4th April. Several hundred miles to the south, Cunningham's men made equally good progress. Having dislodged the Italians from the River Juba on 16th February, Cunningham moved on to Mogadiscio and then to Harar, which fell on 25th March. His advance had been astonishgly rapid – even by the terrifying standards of Blitzkrieg.

With the fall of Massawa and Hara, the claws really began to bite. The rump of Aosta's army was dug in at Amba Alagi, assailed from two sides. The Duke surrendered on 18th May. His capitulation marked the end of large-scale operations in East Africa. The East African campaign had been, in its way, as heartening a success as O'Connor's victory in the Western Desert. And victory in East Africa had been harder-won, for Aosta's troops had fought more energetically than their colleagues in Libya.

Wavell was given no opportunity to rest on his laurels. Under considerable pressure from Churchill, he sent a large quantity of troops from the Western Desert to Greece, where an Italian invasion, in October 1940, had already been beaten off. Greece was less fortunate the second time. On 6th April, powerful German forces poured into Greece and Yugoslavia. Anglo-Greek forces, fighting desperately, were steadily forced back. In the Western Desert, too, the situation worsened dramatically. This sudden and drastic reversal of British fortunes resulted from the arrival in North Africa, during February and March 1941, of the German 5th Light

One of the 380 Italian tanks captured by 7th February

Division (soon renamed 21st Panzer Division), and an officer who, at the time, was little-known; Lieutenant-General Erwin Rommel.

Rommel had been born in 1891 at the small town of Heidenheim in Württemberg. He had served as a company commander in the First World War, and earned considerable acclaim, winning the coveted *Pour le Mérite*. It is interesting to note that even at this early stage in his career, Rommel was an expert on the offensive – brusque, unexpected, and shattering. Between the wars he commanded a regiment of mountain infantry, and was later commandant of the *Kriegsschule* at Wiener Neustadt. He came to Hitler's notice, partly as a result of his book *Infanterie Grieft An* (Infantry in the attack), and spent some time commanding the Führer's escort battalion. In 1940 he led 7th Panzer Division with considerable dash and drive. Blunt and stocky, Rommel was a man of tremendous personal courage and uncanny tactical flair. Historians have not been slow to point out that his grasp of strategy was never particularly firm; he was, nonetheless, an extremely able commander, and a dangerous opponent, very much in his element in the fluid manoeuvres of desert war.

Rommel was under orders from the German High Command to remain on the defensive in Africa, at least until the arrival of 15th Panzer Division, which was expected at the end of May. Once this formation had taken the field, Rommel would be allowed to launch a limited attack in the area of Agedabia, and possibly advance to Benghazi. The Italian *Commando Supremo*, under whose direction Rommel was (at least in theory) to operate, was only too happy to confirm the German decision. While Rommel's troops became acclimatised to desert conditions, the British remained static. Lieutenant-

Rommel, ordered to remain on the defensive until 15th Panzer arrived

General Philip Neame, with a strong covering force, held Western Cyrenaica. The 2nd Armoured Division, less one brigade, and 9th Australian Division, likewise short of one of its brigades, were around Al 'Uqaylah while an Indian motor brigade held Mechili. British Intelligence was aware that German troops had arrived in North Africa, but was quite convinced of *Commando Supremo's* reluctance to move onto the offensive.

When Rommel lunged forward on 31st March the British were, consequently, caught very much off balance. Neame carried out a planned withdrawal, reaching Agedabia on 2nd April, but then things began to go wrong. The destruction of the large petrol dump at Msus on 3rd April worsened an already serious petrol shortage, and severely impeded the mobility of 2nd Armoured Division. Rommel reached Benghazi on 4th

British infantry mop up after the big push into Tobruk

April, but has no intention of halting there. While elements of the Italian Brescia Division pursued the British down the Via Balbia, other formations dashed across the base of the Cyrenaican hump, by-passing the Jebel Achdar. Much of 2nd Armoured Division was cut off, and, to make matters worse, Neame and O'Connor were captured near Derna on the night of 6th-7th March. With Derna and Mechili behind him, and the British army reeling back towards Egypt, Rommel pressed on for Tobruk.

Wavell, urged on by Churchill, decided to hold Tobruk. Accordingly, 7th Australian Division was moved in by sea, in time to deny the town to the Germans. Unable to take Tobruk, Rommel nevertheless continued to advance, and by 10th April Bardia was in German hands and Rommel was across the Egyptian frontier.

Rommel's achievement was, undoubtedly, a remarkable one. It was, though, made possible largely by the fact that one of 2nd Armoured Divis-

ion's brigades, together with numerous aircraft, had been sent to Greece. Cruelly, British military assistance to Greece proved of little value. By 2nd May all British troops had been evacuated from Greece, whose government had been forced to surrender. Most of the troops from Greece were shipped to Crete, which was itself attacked on 20th May. After a courageous defence, Crete too fell. Many of the garrison were taken off by sea, though at heavy cost to the Royal Navy. In the desert, Rommel's star remained in the ascendant. A British limited counteroffensive in mid-May met with little success, and the more ambitious Operation Battleaxe, 15th-17th June, failed.

The dismal result of Battleaxe sealed Wavell's fate. Churchill decided to replace him by General Sir Claude Auchinleck, C-in-C in India. The wisdom of this decision is open to question. Auchinleck, though an excellent general, was infinitely more at home in India than in the desert. It might also be argued that the dismissal of Wavell was itself somewhat unreasonable, since he had launched Battleaxe only on Churchill's insistence, against his own better judgement.

A general reorganisation of British forces in the Middle East took place following Auchinleck's assumption of command. In the north, General Maitland Wilson was given command of the newly-formed Ninth Army, with Palestine and Transjordan as its 'Base and Lines of Communication Area'. In the Western Desert, General Sir Alan Cunningham, fresh from his success against the Italians in East Africa, took over Eighth Army, with Wilson's old command, 'British Troops in Egypt', as his 'Base and Lines of Communication Area'. Eighth Army was divided into two corps.

The old Western Desert Force be-

31st March. Rommel strikes back. The British lose many prisoners and are sent reeling towards Egypt

came XIII Corps, under Lieutenant-General A R Godwin-Austin. A new corps, to be numbered XXX, was in process of formation. This was to contain much of the available armour, and its first commander, Lieutenant-General Pope, had just finished a tour of duty as Director of Armoured Fighting Vehicles. Unfortunately, Pope was killed in a plane crash on 5th October, and was replaced by Major-General C W M Norrie. Towards the end of October, both corps HQ moved out into the desert, and prepared for an offensive against the Axis forces.

Auchinleck had been under pressure from Churchill to move into the attack ever since he took over command in the Middle East. It was Auchinleck's view, however, that there was no point in mounting an offensive unless his forces were sufficiently strong. He was confronted by a two-fold problem. He had, firstly, to obtain sufficient equipment, particularly armour, to permit the engagement of Rommel on favourable terms. Secondly, he had to ensure that the formations comprising Eighth Army had reached an adequate standard of training before committing them to an attack. On 18th November, Cunningham's army swept forward in Operation Crusader, the long-awaited counteroffensive. The advance went well at first, but was soon interrupted by a bold, hooking, counterthrust, delivered by Rommel at the head of 15th and 21st Panzer Divisions. This produced considerable alarm – not to say panic – among the British. Cunningham decided to fall back and regroup, but was prevented from doing so by Auchinleck who, quite rightly under the circumstances, replaced Cunningham by Major-General N M Ritchie. The battle continued, both sides fighting with remarkable ferocity. Ritchie correctly believed that Rommel was at his last gasp, and renewed the attack. His resolution was well rewarded. Heavily punished, the Axis forces fell back.

General Sir Claude Auchinleck. Replaced Wavell as C-in-C after June 1941

Tobruk was relieved, and the advance went on, past the Jebel 'Achdar, to Benghazi and beyond.

In the second week of January 1942, Rommel's battered forces concentrated around Mersa Brega. His staff worked out that, despite overall British strength, there was a slight German supremacy in armour in Western Cyrenaica. Moreover, the battle-hardened 7th Armoured Division was recuperating south of Tobruk, while the 1st Armoured Division, unused to desert conditions, covered the British front near Agedabia. The latter piece of information persuaded Rommel to counterattack, and to do so rapidly, before more British armour moved into Cyrenaica. On 21st January Rommel turned on the over-extended Eighth Army. The experienced and self-confident soldiers of 15th Panzer lacerated the green troops of 1st Armoured Division. Benghazi fell on 29th January, and Ritchie decided to give up the Cyrenaica hump, and to fall back to Gazala.

Tobruk. By the end of December it was once more in British hands

5th October. Norrie takes over XXX Corps from Pope

Ritchie takes over Eighth Army from Cunningham

The Gazala line

Following its expulsion from Western Cyrenaica, Eighth Army established itself in a series of positions forming the Gazala Line. While both sides prepared for a renewal of the struggle, there was a four-month lull in which peace, of a sort, descended upon the scarred surface of the desert. The fighting during the winter of 1941-42 had shown up several serious defects in the organisation of Eighth Army, and Auchinleck capitalised upon the pause to make several neccessary changes.

It was lamentably obvious that cooperation between armour and infantry within Eighth Army left much to be desired. Whereas the German Panzergrenadiers worked closely with their tanks, there was an alarming tendency for British infantry and armour to fight separate battles and thus incur defeat in detail. Many of the lessons of 1940 had gone unlearned; British commanders failed to concentrate their armour, and often employed it with hesitancy.

In an effort to produce an answer to the well-integrated, hard-hitting Panzer divisions, a new standard form of armoured division was evolved. From now on, an armoured division would, on paper, contain an armoured brigade group, consisting of three tank regiments, one motor infantry battalion and a field and anti-tank artillery regiment, together with a motor brigade group, which would be composed of three motor infantry battalions and an artillery regiment. Both types of brigade would also include engineers, signals, and light anti-aircraft elements. The army tank brigades, each of which contained three regiments of slow 'I' tanks, would not be included in the armoured divisions, but would be allocated as required. Infantry divisions, too, were reorganised. Each division would now contain three brigade groups. These

Rommel's infantry and armour move up to the Gazala Line, established by the Allies in the lull before May 1942

70

The German PzKw III (with 5cm short barrelled gun). *Crew:* five. *Weight:* 22 tons.
Speed: 11mph (cross country) and 25mph (road). *Range:* 60 miles (cross country)
and 109 miles (road). *Length:* 17 feet 9 inches. *Width:* 9 feet 7 inches. *Height:*
8 feet 3 inches. *Engine:* one Maybach HL 120 petrol engine, 300bhp. *Armament:*
one 5cm KwK L/42 gun with 99 rounds and two 7.92mm machine guns with 2,000
rounds. *Armour:* 30mm nose, driver's plate, sides and turret front, sides and rear,
21mm hull rear, 17mm hull top, 16mm belly and 10mm turret top

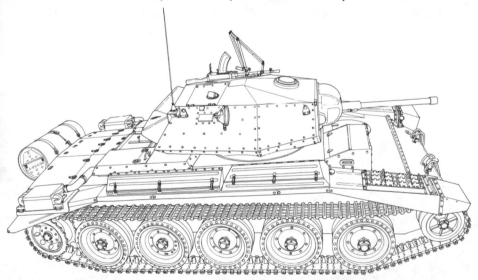

The British Cruiser Tank Mark VI, Crusader. Illustrated is a Crusader III, an upgunned
version of the earlier models, which had 2-pounders as their main armament.
Crew: three. *Weight:* 19¾ tons. *Speed:* 27mph. *Range:* 100 miles. *Length:* 19 feet
8 inches. *Width:* 8 feet 8 inches. *Height:* 7 feet 4 inches. *Engine:* Nuffield-built
Liberty petrol engine, 340bhp. *Armament:* one 6-pounder (2.25-inch) gun and one
Besa machine gun. *Armour:* 7mm minimum and 51mm maximum

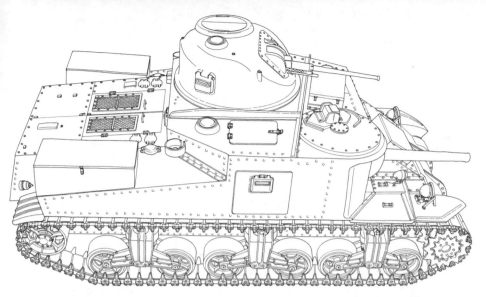

The American M3 General Lee/Grant tank was the first US medium tank to see
service with the British army, and its arrival in the Western Desert was greeted with
considerable enthusiasm, for in the Grant the armoured forces for the first time had
a machine that could take on German tanks and anti-tank units on something like an
equal footing. The original General Lee version was the basic American design, and
this had an extra cupola above the turret, mounting a machine gun. The General
Grant had a turret of British design and manufacture, and this did away with the
upper cupola. The one main drawback of the Lee/Grant was the fact that the main
armament was in the hull and had only a limited traverse. Illustrated is a Mk 1,
distinguishable by its rivetted hull. It was a well-armoured type, and also reasonably
fast and very reliable. *Weight:* 28.5 tons. *Crew:* six. *Speed:* 26mph (road). *Range:*
144 miles maximum. *Length:* 18 feet 6 inches. *Width:* 8 feet 11 inches. *Height:*
10 feet 4 inches. *Engine:* one Continental R-975 air-cooled radial engine, 340bhp.
Armament: one 75mm M2 L/31 gun with 41 rounds (traverse 60 degrees), one 37mm
M5 L/50 with 179 rounds (traverse 360 degrees) and up to three .3-inch Browning
machine guns with 6,000 rounds. *Armour:* 2 inches hull upper nose, glacis plate and
driver's plate and turret front, sides and rear. $1\frac{1}{2}$ inches hull sides and upper rear,
1 inch front belly and turret roof and $\frac{1}{2}$ inch lower rear, engine covers and rear belly.
The 37mm gun was the first in a tank to be fitted with a stabilising gear

General Grants, with which the British were re-equipping early in 1942

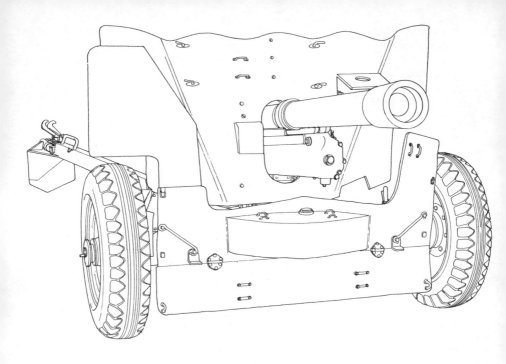

A German 88mm anti-aircraft gun, dramatically successful against tanks

The basic anti-tank weapon with which Great Britain went to war was the 2-pounder, which, theoretically, was capable of piercing the armour of any German tank at a range of 1,200 yards. The drawback, however, was that the solid shot fired by the 2-pounder broke up on hitting the face-hardened armour used by the Germans. This problem became more acute as the Germans continued to up-armour their tanks as the result of war experience. Thus the British developed the 6-pounder anti-tank gun illustrated, to try to put themselves ahead of the latest German armour. First work had begun in 1938, and the failing of the 2-pounder explained above led to the new gun being given a very high priority. But because of the need to re-equip the army in Britain after Dunkirk, the 2-pounder was retained in production to save time, thereby further delaying the 6-pounder. By mid-1942, the Eighth Army had only 112 of the newer guns. *Crew:* five. *Weight:* 2,560lbs. *Range:* 5,000 yards. *Calibre:* 2.25 inches. *Length of barrel:* 43 calibres. *Overall length of gun:* 101 inches. *Weight of shot:* 6lbs 4½oz (HE could also be fired, but was in very short supply). *Muzzle velocity:* 2,800 feet per second. *Armour penetration:* 81mm at 500 yards at 30 degrees

infantry brigade groups consisted of three infantry battalions and an artillery regiment, with engineer, signals, and light anti-aircraft backing. Artillery regiments, it should be noted, were reorganised into hybrid field/anti-tank units, each of which comprised three field batteries (each of eight 25-pounder guns) and one anti-tank battery (of sixteen anti-tank guns). The existing anti-tank regiments were to be split up to form this fourth battery.

The battles of 1941 and early 1942 had demonstrated the qualitative inferiority of much British equipment. The main German tank during those years was the Panzer Mark III. This vehicle had originally mounted a 37mm gun, but all those sent to North Africa had been re-equipped with the more powerful short 50mm weapon. Many of these tanks had been up-armoured by the addition of extra plates of hardened steel, greatly increasing their effectiveness in combat. It was, in fact, almost impossible for the 2-pounder guns of the British 'I' tanks or Crusaders to penetrate these reinforced Mark IIIs. During the summer of 1942 the Afrika Korps received a number of Mark III 'specials' and Mark IVs. The former carried a long 50mm gun, while the latter carried the lethal 75mm piece.

Relatively few of these useful tanks, though, were available at the time of the Gazala battles.

To counter these dependable and hard-hitting fighting vehicles, the British were in process of re-equipping with a new, very effective, tank. This was the American 'General Grant', which mounted a 75mm gun in a sponson on the hull, and a 37mm in the turret. The Grant's main armament was certainly an improvement on previous British tank guns, but its location, low down on the vehicle's body, made for awkward tactical handling; it was impossible for the tank to fire its main armament from the hull-down position. Furthermore, the 75mm gun was basically a field-piece, good for firing a high explosive round, but with only a moderate armour-piercing capability. Nevertheless, the Grant compared more than favourably with the slow 'I' tanks, with their heavy armour but light guns, the fragile Crusaders, and the light Stuarts.

The Germans again held the advantage as far as anti-tank weapons were concerned. One of the most dramatically successful weapons to emerge from the Second World War was the 88mm anti-aircraft gun, used in an anti-tank rôle. This weapon's high muzzle velocity gave it a flat trajec-

75

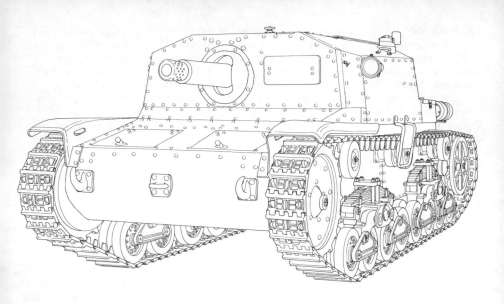

The armour used by Italy at the time she entered the war was on the whole ill-suited to desert conditions and in many instances obsolete. But by the beginning of 1942, the Italians were producing improved armoured vehicles, one of which was the M75/18 Semovente (self-propelled gun). This entered service with the Ariete Division in the spring of 1942. *Weight:* 12 tons. *Crew:* four. *Speed:* 20.5mph maximum. *Armament:* one 75mm gun and one 6.5mm machine gun. The 75mm gun had a maximum range of 10,280 yards, a rate of fire of four rounds per minute. In the 75/18 it has an elevation of from −11 degrees to +22.5 degrees and a traverse of 17 degrees left and 20 degrees right

tory and excellent penetrating power; it was deadly against all types of British armour. It had, admittedly, disadvantages; its high silhouette made it difficult to conceal, and it was notoriously vulnerable to high explosive fire. The main British anti-tank gun had, for some time, been the 2-pounder, though this was being steadily replaced by the more effective 6-pounder – though there were only 112 of the latter weapons in service with Eighth Army by mid-1942. The standard British field gun, the solidly reliable 25-pounder, could, and, indeed, all too often had to be, used as an anti-tank weapon.

Italian equipment was, on the whole, obsolete and not particularly well-suited to the trying conditions of desert warfare. The Italian M 13/40 tank, with its pitifully thin armour

and its 40mm gun, was widely referred to as the 'Mobile coffin'. The M 14/41 was an improved version with a larger engine, but it retained its predecessor's brisk combustible potential. Of much better quality was the M 75/18 *Semovente*, a self-propelled gun with a range of over 10,000 yards.

By May 1942 the Gazala Line was a position of considerable strength. Eighth Army continued to be divided into two corps. Lieutenant-General W H E Gott's XIII Corps contained the bulk of the infantry, and garrisoned the main defensive line. In the north, with its right flank touching the sea just west of the village of Gazala, lay Major-General D H Pienaar's 1st South African Division, with three brigades in line. To the south of Pienaar's command, the front was held by Major-General W H

Ramsden's 50th (Northumbrian) Division. 50th Division, too, had its three brigades – 151st, 69th and 150th – in the line from Alem Hamaz to Sidi Muftah. Tobruk, an important administrative centre, lay thirty miles behind the Gazala Line. Its defence was entrusted to Major-General H B Klopper and the 2nd South African Division, with 9th Indian Infantry Brigade attached. The town itself was held by the Indian brigade and the 4th South African Brigade; Klopper's remaining South African Brigade, the 6th, covered the area between Tobruk and Gazala.

Lieutenant-General C W H Norrie's XXX Corps, made up of 1st and 7th Armoured Divisions, 29th Indian Infantry Brigade and 1st Free French Brigade, was posted to the left rear of the main Gazala positions. Major-General H Lumsden's 1st Armoured Division had one of its armoured brigades, the 22nd, on the Trigh El Abd near Bir el Harmat, and the other, the 2nd, astride the Trigh Capuzzo near Bir Lefa. Lumsden's infantry element, 201st Guards Brigade, was securely established in a defensive 'box' at Knightsbridge, the junction of the Trigh Capuzzo and the Trigh Bir Hacheim. 7th Armoured Division watched the army's southern flank. Major-General F W Messervy's HQ lay just south of the Trigh el Abd, at Bir Beuid, and his only armoured brigade, the 4th, lay slightly west of this. Messervy had two motor brigades under command. 7th Motor Brigade was based on a box at Retma, and 3rd Indian Motor Brigade operated some fifteen miles to the west. Both these motor brigades patrolled actively, sending out columns as far as Rotonda Segnali. In addition to these patrols, screening and reconnaissance was carried out by the armoured cars of the King's Dragoon Guards, 12th Lancers, and two South African armoured car regiments.

At the southern end of the Gazala Line, just over forty miles, as the crow flies, from the sea, lay the old caravanning centre of Bir Hacheim, held by Brigadier-General Koenig's 1st Free French Brigade. This formation's presence in the line was the result of a protracted high-level struggle between de Gaulle and the British High Command. On 20th September 1941 de Gaulle had approved the composition of two Free French 'light divisions' – equal, in British terms, to brigade groups. Early in October de Gaulle wrote to both Churchill and Auchinleck, informing them of Free French resources in the Middle East, and expressing a desire for large-scale French participation in the desert war. On 27th November, General Ismay, Chief of Staff to the War Cabinet, replied to de Gaulle, pointing out that Free French units were widely dispersed, and had not been trained to fight as brigades. De Gaulle was, predictably, picqued by British rejection of his offer of assistance. He made a renewed offer to the Russians, stating that if Free French troops were not to be employed in Libya, then he was perfectly prepared to use them on the Eastern Front. The Franco-Russian negotiations helped bring about a British change of heart. On 7th December Churchill wrote to de Gaulle that he had 'just heard from General Auchinleck that he is most anxious to use a Free French brigade immediately in the Cyrenaican operations'.

Koenig's brigade moved into Libya in December, and stayed briefly at Duba camp, some thirty miles west of Mersa Matruh. They went into action on 15th January 1942, at Halfaya. The Axis garrison of Halfaya, elements of the Savona Division, and a battalion of 104th Panzer Grenadier Regiment, under the command of General Georgis, had been cut off, following the British capture of Sollum and Bardia. Georgis's encircled troops put up a resolute defence, but were forced to surrender on 17th January. The Free French Brigade followed the British advance westwards, but was employed, to its annoyance, in minor mopping-

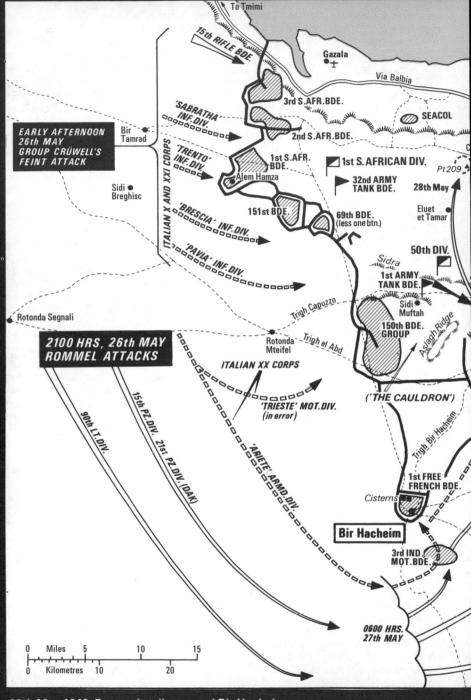

26th May 1942. Rommel strikes round Bir Hacheim

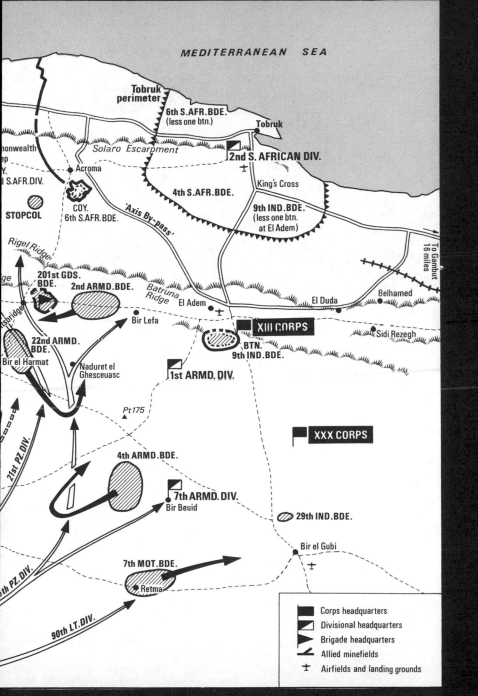

MEDITERRANEAN SEA

Tobruk perimeter

6th S.AFR.BDE.
(less one btn.)

Tobruk

nonwealth
ep

Solaro Escarpment

2nd S. AFRICAN DIV.

S.AFR.DIV.

Acroma

King's Cross

4th S.AFR.BDE.

9th IND.BDE.
(less one btn.
at El Adem)

STOPCOL

COY.
6th S.AFR.BDE.

'Axis By-pass'

To Gambut
16 miles

Rigel Ridge

201st GDS.
BDE.

2nd ARMD.BDE.

Batruna
Ridge

El Adem

El Duda

Belhamed

ge

Bir Lefa

XIII CORPS

Sidi Rezegh

tsbridge

22nd ARMD.
BDE.

Bir el Harmat

Naduret el
Ghesceuasc

1st ARMD. DIV.

BTN.
9th IND.BDE.

21st PZ.DIV.

Pt 175

XXX CORPS

4th ARMD.BDE.

7th ARMD.DIV.
Bir Beuid

29th IND.BDE.

Bir el Gubi

7th MOT.BDE.

th PZ.DIV.

Retma

90th LT.DIV.

Corps headquarters

Divisional headquarters

Brigade headquarters

Allied minefields

Airfields and landing grounds

up operations and the like. When, after Rommel's *volte face* of 21st January, the pendulum swung in the favour of the Axis, Koenig's men joined the rest of Eighth Army around Gazala, and, on 14th February, took over Bir Hacheim from the Yorkshiremen of 150th Infantry Brigade.

The Bir Hacheim box was, like the remainder of the Gazala positions, surrounded by minefields. The front of the Gazala Line formed a huge mine marsh, containing over 500,000 anti-tank mines. The mine belt ran southwards from Gazala to Bir Hacheim. It then curled back north north-east, forming, in effect, a V to the north of Koenig's position. A serious flaw in Eighth Army's defensive plan was that a large portion of the minefield was not covered by fire. An unguarded obstacle is no obstacle; events were to demonstrate the unwisdom of entrusting a large part of the British front to the latent deadliness of mines.

Across several miles of ragged desert to the west lay Rommel. The German general was nominally subordinated to General Bastico, the Italian C-in-C in North Africa. In practice, though, Bastico exercised little control over the impetuous Rommel. Rommel's command had been renamed *Panzerarmee Afrika* on 22nd January. Its German element was General Crüwell's *Deutches Afrika Korps* (DAK), made up of 15th and 21st Panzer Divisions and 90th Light Division. This was the cutting edge of *Panzerarmee Afrika*. It was supported by Italian formations whose standards of training, equipment and morale differed sharply from one another. It should not be assumed that all Italian formations were uniformly bad; some, it is true, showed a distressing lack of fighting spirit, but others proved worthy counterparts to the tough divisions of the DAK. The best of the Italian formations was XX Corps, which contained the Ariete Armoured Division and the Trieste Motorised Division. Of less reliable quality were the other two Italian corps, X Corps, containing the Brescia and Pavia Infantry Divisions, and XXI Corps, with the Sabratha and Trento Divisions.

Rommel's stormy relations with his Italian allies caused him considerable worry and frustration. He was, though, bedevilled by a more serious prob-

Left : Colonial machine gunners of Koenig's 1st Free French Brigade
Above and below : The unending stream of Italian prisoners

lem. If the British supply situation was difficult, Rommel's was perilous. Although Axis supply routes, from Sicily and Naples to Tripoli and Benghazi, were short, they were vulnerable to air and submarine attack. Shortage of fuel was Rommel's greatest concern. Roughly 120,000 tons of fuel were needed every month to keep *Panzerarmee Afrika* in fully operational condition. In November 1941 only 80,000 tons of fuel were sent off, and of this, only 30,000 tons arrived in Africa, the remainder having fallen victim to British aircraft, submarines and surface vessels.

The island of Malta provided the British with a useful base for operations against Axis convoys, and as such was a notable threat to Rommel's security. In January 1942 *Luftflotte II* arrived in Sicily, and stepped up the air attack on Malta. As a result, over 60,000 tons of fuel got through to Africa that month, with no loss. In April, month of the great air effort against Malta, 150,000 tons of fuel reached Rommel's forces. Axis losses in Operation Crusader had been substantial; on 5th December Rommel informed his Italian superiors that he had only forty tanks left. To the credit of the Italians, they made every effort to rectify this deficiency. On 19th December, four Italian cargo ships arrived at Tripoli, bringing two squadrons of armour, a battery of artillery, and numerous other supplies. To ensure its safe passage across the Mediterranean, this convoy had been escorted by a battleship, three cruisers and twelve destroyers. On 5th January a new convoy disgorged fifty-five tanks and twenty armoured cars.

The British supply and reinforcement situation, though far from favourable, was by no means as depressing as that which faced the Axis. Supplies from Britain were sent round the Cape and through the Suez canal, and some equipment took the swifter Takoradi air route. Although the Red Sea was within range of German aircraft operating from southern Greece, delays thus imposed were slight. To improve transport to the front line, the British extended the Alexandria-Mersa Matruh railway as far as Fort Capuzzo, and later up to Belhamed. Huge advanced supply bases were established at Tobruk, Belhamed and Jarabub. Useful though these bases were, they were to prove an extra defensive consideration for British commanders.

The question of Malta thrust Axis planners onto the horns of a dilemma. British presence in Malta threatened Axis supply routes, preventing an adequate build-up in the desert. If, however, a serious effort were to be made against Malta, this would absorb much of the air power essential to the conduct of operations in Africa. Furthermore, an airborne assault on Malta would certainly result in very heavy casualties for the attackers; German experience of airborne operations in Crete served to emphasise this unpalatable fact. At the end of April 1942, Mussolini, accompanied by Cavallero, Chief of the Italian General Staff, visited Hitler at Obersalzburg to discuss strategy in the Middle East. Cavallero advocated an attack on Malta (Operation Hercules), to be carried out prior to an advance into Egypt (Operation Aida). He was opposed by Field-Marshal Kesselring, who, as C-in-C South, was responsible for coordinating German efforts in the Mediterranean theatre. The conference's eventual decision was that Hercules should be postponed until after Rommel had attacked the British in Cyrenaica and captured Tobruk. Having accomplished this, Rommel would then stand on the defensive on the Egyptian frontier while a major Axis assault fell on Malta. Once the island had been occupied, Aida would proceed to its conclusion, the occupation of Egypt.

Working under these strategic guidelines, Rommel drew up his plans for Operation Venezia, the offensive against the British in Cyrenaica. The resultant project was typical of

Above: A party of Germans examine a captured tank, a fragile Crusader
Below: A German 50mm anti-tank gun moves up to the Gazala Line

Rommel; it was bold, uncomplicated, and based on gross underestimation of his opponents. In simple terms, Rommel proposed to pin the British by a frontal attack on the Gazala Line, while his motorised elements swung widely round the desert flank and ripped into Eighth Army's rear. *Gruppe* Crüwell, consisting of the Italian X and XXI Corps, strengthened by the German 15th Rifle Brigade, was to launch a holding attack on the portion of the Gazala Line held by 1st South African Division and 50th Division. Under cover of this demonstration, Rommel himself would lead his main striking force on a broad right hook to the south of the Gazala Line. This shock force was to consist of the DAK, now commanded by General Nehring in place of Crüwell, together with the Italian XX Corps.

The initial plan called for an early capture of Bir Hacheim, and an advance through that location. In the final version of the plan, most of Rommel's force was to skirt Bir Hacheim to the south; Ariete would deal with the position itself. Major-General von Mellenthin, who at the

Above: Field-Marshal Kesselring, German C-in-C South, responsible for the Mediterranean theatre. *Below:* Auchinleck and Ritchie at Eighth Army HQ, June 1942. *Right:* Rommel meets Nehring in Tunisia after the latter succeeded Crüwell as CO *Afrika Korps*

New Me 109s (above), superior to the Hurricane (below) which together with Kittyhawks made up most of the greatly inferior Allied air strength

time was Chief of Staff of Crüwell, observed that 'our attitude to Bir Hacheim was far too casual . . . the capture of the place was a *sine qua non* for any successful operation behind the Gazala Line. Once our main armoured forces had gone round, Bir Hacheim was in a position to serve as a base for attacks on our supply convoys, and in fact it did so very effectively. In my opinion both 90th Light and the Italian Armoured Corps should have attacked Bir Hacheim on the first day of the assault, with strong Luftwaffe support.' Having passed south of Bir Hacheim, Rommel planned to swing north and strike into the Acroma area, while 90th Light and some armoured reconnaissance units pushed on towards El Adem. The objective of Acroma for the first day was remarkably ambitious, and presupposed complete lack of response on the part of the British High Command.

On 20th May Auchinleck suggested to Ritchie that Rommel's most likely line of attack was along the Trigh Capuzzo, on 50th Division's front. Auchinleck went on to add, however, that a flanking attack was by no means impossible. He advised Ritchie to concentrate his armour on the Trigh Capuzzo, and recommended that the armoured divisions should be kept intact and not be committed to battle piecemeal. Unfortunately for the British, Ritchie and his divisional commanders paid little heed to the latter portion of Auchinleck's advice.

Throughout 26th May, Rommel's army moved up to its concentration area east of Rotonda Segnali. Rommel had at his disposal some 90,000 men, backed by 560 tanks, 332 of which were German. The Luftwaffe was present in strength; there were just under 500 serviceable German and Italian aircraft flying in support of Rommel's assault. In and behind the Gazala defences were the 100,000 men of Eighth Army, with no less than 849 tanks, 167 of them Grants. Although Ritchie outnumbered Rommel on the ground, the air balance was swung heavily in the latter's favour, for the Desert Air Force had only 190 serviceable aircraft, most of them Kittyhawks and Hurricanes, somewhat inferior to the new Me 109F.

Bir Hacheim

The ground over which the Gazala battles were fought was, like the rest of the Western Desert, arid and sandy, intersected by sharp ridges. Numerous tracks, of differing quality, criss-crossed the battlefield. Along the coast ran the Via Balbia, a well-surfaced road of Italian construction. As the road neared Tobruk, a switch known as Axis By-Pass skirted the town's defences. The remaining tracks were rather less good, lacking metalled surfaces, and marked by lines of rusting oil-drums. Parallel to the Via Balbia, and some ten to fifteen miles to the south, ran the Trigh Capuzzo, which pursued its bumpy course from Rotonda Mteifel to Sollum. From Rotonda Mteifel, too, ran the Trigh el Abd, which curled away south-east, through Bir el Gubi. Two ridge systems broke the monotony of the desert. A few miles from the sea was a coastal escarpment, where the ground rose abruptly from the narrow litoral plain. To the south lay a second line of high ground, forming Sidra, Rigel and Batruna ridges. Five miles south of Sidra ridge, and at an angle to it, lay Aslagh ridge. From the map, the area seems alive with place names. Tobruk, in fact was the only town; apart from a few Arab villages near the coast, the names which look so imposing on the map simply mark an ancient tomb or long-disused cistern.

Bir Hacheim itself lay at a track junction. One track, the Trigh Bir Hacheim, ran towards Acroma and the sea, while another headed towards El Adem and Tobruk. Other tracks curved off to the south-east, to Bir el Gubi and Retma. Bir Hacheim certainly made no concessions to the Hollywood image of an oasis. It was simply an undulating patch of desert, with only two features to mark it out as different from the desert which rolled away on either side. One of these landmarks was a small fort, a

Gazala. A damaged tank in the dense network of lorry and tank tracks

90

A Free French Foreign Legionnaire

white, rectangular structure in the best Beau Geste style. Two miles north-west of the fort were the two old cisterns which gave Bir Hacheim its name. The cisterns were broken and partially covered with sand; Koenig's men, with Gallic zest, referred to them as 'Les Mamelles'. A low, barely perceptible, ridge ran between the fort and the cisterns. Unimpressive though it appeared, Bir Hachiem was a position of prime tactical importance. It commanded the last piece of useful terrain before the Great Libyan Sand Sea, and provided an anchor for the southern flank of the Gazala Line.

The 1st Free French Brigade had relieved 150th Infantry Brigade at Bir Hacheim on 14th February. Koenig's brigade was a mixture of nationalities. Lieutenant-Colonel Amilakvari, of Georgian extraction, commanded the 2nd and 3rd Battalions of the Foreign Legion. These units were well under

strength, numbering just over 500 all told. From central Africa came the 2nd *Bataillon de Marche de l'Oubanghi Chari*, under Lieutenant-Colonel de Roux and Major Amiel. It is difficult to give a precise translation of the term *Bataillon de Marche*. The phrase denotes a unit raised on an *ad hoc* basis, often for a special purpose; in this instance it is best left untranslated. Lieutenant-Colonel Broché led the *Bataillon du Pacifique*, recruited in French colonies in the South Seas. The 1st Battalion of *Infanterie de la Marine*, under Major Savey, was split up; one of its companies was attached to each of the other infantry battalions, and Savey himself commanded the brigade's rear echelon. It should be noted in passing that *Infanterie de la Marine* should not be thought of as marines in the normal sense of the word; they were, properly

A Foreign Legionnaire from Senegal, at Bir Hacheim

Pipe-smoking Free French patrol. Koenig's brigade of Frenchmen, Africans and Legionnaires was 3,600-strong

speaking, colonial infantry. There were, though, marines at Bir Hacheim. Lieutenant - Commander Amyot d'Inville and the men of the 1st *Fusiliers-Marins* provided the brigade with anti-aircraft defence. Koenig had his own artillery, in the form of Major Laurent-Champrosay's 1st Artillery Regiment. The brigade also included the 22nd North African Company, led by Captain Lequesne, and Captain Jacquin's 2nd Anti-Tank Company. Engineer and signals detachments, and a large medical team, completed Koenig's establishment.

The defenders of Bir Hacheim were equipped with a mixture of British and French material. The 1st Artillery had the well-tried *soixante-quinze*, the effective and fast firing 75mm field gun. These guns had been brought from Syria, and had been refitted in the workshops at Beirut. They were organised in four batteries, each with six guns. The brigade was particularly well-provided with anti-tank guns. There were eighteen 25mm, seven 47mm and thirty 75mm anti-tank weapons, together with forty-six anti-tank rifles of rather doubtful effectiveness. The *Fusiliers-Marins* had two quadruple 13.2mm anti-aircraft guns, and twelve 40mm Bofors guns. A British detachment – the only British troops at Bir Hacheim – manned six more Bofors guns. D'Inville's men received their Bofors while in position at Bir Hacheim, and were given instruction in their use by Captain Tomkins, commander of the British anti-aircraft section. Tomkins also served as Koenig's liaison officer. Within the position were forty-four

mortars, twenty of them 81mm and the remainder 60mm. These were manned by the infantry battalions. It appears that seven old Italian 47mm guns and two British 25-pounders had been left on the position by 150th Brigade; these weapons, too, were put into service by the French. Besides numerous lorries and guntowers, the brigade had sixty-three Bren-carriers. These were lightly armoured, tracked vehicles, mounting a light machine gun.

Koenig's force was made up of men of vastly differing backgrounds, training and outlook. This illustrates the way in which Free France appealed to a varied cross-section of the French army, and indeed, the population as a whole. The officers of the brigade represented both dedicated career officers, often from old military families, and men who had joined Free France in 1940 with little or no military experience. There were examples of most shades of the political spectrum. Major Jacques Savey, for example, who commanded the *Infan-*

terie *de la Marine,* had been a Dominican at the Haute Djezireh mission in Syria. He had rallied to de Gaulle in 1940, and had been promoted rapidly. At the other extreme was a Lieutenant Dewey, a fiery individual whose left-wing political views sometimes alarmed his superiors. The brigade had been in existence for only a relatively short time; its component units had come from several sources by very different routes. Most of the *Fusiliers-Marins* had got away to Britain from Dunkirk, and had decided to soldier-on with de Gaulle rather than return to France.

The Legion battalions contained volunteers from several countries – including, incidentally, Germany. Lieutenant-Colonel Broché was a regular officer; in 1940, as a captain, he had persuaded Tahiti to rally to Free France with its autonomous company of colonial infantry. This company formed the nucleus of Broché's *Bataillon du Pacifique.* The *Bataillon de Marche* had already distinguished itself. Raised in Oubanghi, Chad and the Congo, it had crossed Africa in lorries and joined in the British attack on Keren. Many of the officers in the colonial battalions were French civil servants and settlers, who had joined the Free French and

Left: Legionnaires in the Jebel Druze
Below: One of Koenig's sixty-three Bren-carriers patrols near the oasis of Bir Hacheim – far from the Hollywood image of an oasis

obtained commissions. The high casualty rate among officers in the Free French army is illustrated by the fate of Koenig's battalion commanders. Lieutenant-Colonel Amilakvari, the quiet Georgian, was killed at El Alamein. Lieutenant-Colonel de Roux of the *Bataillon de Marche* died in an air crash, while Broché was killed by a shell at Bir Hacheim. The popular Amyot d'Inville – nicknamed 'the admiral' – and Laurent Champrosay of the artillery were both killed in the Italian campaign.

The 1st Free French Brigade, on arrival at Bir Hacheim, numbered about 3,600 officers and men. French sources give numerous different figures for the size of the brigade, and, indeed for its casualties. It seems likely, though, that while Koenig's command was in fact larger than 3,600, many of his troops would have been employed in the brigade's rear echelon. Koenig's immediate task was to improve the defences of Bir Hacheim. The position lay at the southern end of the great 'mine marsh' which covered Eighth Army's front. This was already in existence when the brigade moved into position. The position around Bir Hacheim was extended and thickened up by French efforts. Smaller minefields were laid around the defensive perimeter, inside the area of the main mine marsh. Most of the mines were of the anti-tank variety, designed to explode under the weight of a vehicle, but to allow men on foot to pass over safely. Some barbed wire was strung round the position, but little attention was paid to this, as the greatest threat was likely to come from tanks rather than infantry. More than 50,000 mines were laid by the French. Three gaps were left in the minefields, to allow the garrison to enter and leave. These openings were situated on the northeast, south-east and north-west sides of the defences. Each of these entrances was narrow and could be closed rapidly in an attack.

Behind the minefield, the French infantry took up their positions. The eastern sector was held by the 2nd Battalion of the Legion. The *Bataillon de Marche* occupied the north-west, while the *Bataillon du Pacifique* held the south-west. Koenig's command post was located centrally. Anti-tank guns were sited to cover the entrances, with arcs of fire interlocking over the minefields. Considerable attention was paid to the construction of field fortifications. It is often said that the French soldier suffers from a great unwillingness to dig in. This was certainly not so at Bir Hacheim; Koenig's men dug like moles. As the weeks went by, the surface of the desert became honeycombed with fire trenches, dugouts and command posts. The depth and diversity of these defence works was to have an important effect on the coming battle.

The Bir Hacheim position closely resembled the defensive boxes employed by several other British formations in the Gazala Line. In many respects, the whole philosophy of the box system is open to question. History shows that a static defence has little chance of long-term success. Yet the garrisons of the boxes settled down to what was, all too often, a brave but totally unenterprising defensive battle. Koenig was aware of the dangers of surrendering the initiative; perhaps the painful memory of the Maginot Line served to emphasise this. He was also aware of the necessity of covering minefields with fire. So as not to sacrifice the mobility of his brigade, Koenig split the 3rd Battalion of the Legion into patrols and motorised columns. During the four-month lull in major operations, Koenig formed several semi-independent combat groups, each of which consisted of one or two companies of lorried infantry, some 75s, light anti-tank guns, and an anti-aircraft detachment. These columns operated some distance from Bir Hacheim, and proved extremely useful for raiding, obtaining information from the Arabs, and minelaying. A standing patrol,

Above : British Sappers add to the extensive minefields shielding Bir Hacheim
Below : A French patrol cautiously approaches a German half-track which
it has just fired on and damaged

under Captain de Lamaze of the Legion, watched the 'V' in the main minebelt north of Bir Hacheim. Lamaze had under his command a detachment of the 3rd Battalion of the Legion, three 75s, and three Bren carrier sections, led by Lieutenant Dewey and Cadet Officers Bourdis and Maury, together with some signallers and engineers.

By the end of March most of the work on the defences of Bir Hacheim had been completed. Mobile patrols made forays into No-Man's Land and behind the German lines. Rations arrived regularly; it even proved possible to send troops to the coast near Tobruk for a swim at a spot which soon became known as 'Koenig's beach'. Towards the middle of April there was some talk of replacing the French garrison with a South African Brigade. Some South African officers came forward to reconnoitre the position with a view to taking it over, but the scheme was dropped due to a renewal of enemy activity. On 18th May – dangerously late – the Bofors guns arrived, and the *Fusiliers-Marins* set about learning how to operate them. The *Fusiliers-Marins* did not have the pleasure of a passing-out parade, but their final examination was to be disturbingly realistic.

From 15th May onwards Koenig received frequent warnings from HQ 7th Armoured Division of an imminent Axis offensive. The influx of supplies was stepped up; by mid-May there were 20,000 75mm rounds on the position. Reports were rife that the Germans had recently used poison gas in Russia; Koenig accordingly ordered that gas masks should be carried. Beards were shaved off, and the troops performed gas mask drill – hardly the most congenial of occupations in the scorching desert heat. Recreational visits to Tobruk were stopped. With firm morale, and confidence in their leaders and their allies, the men of the 1st Free French Brigade awaited the coming assault with calm resolution.

Koenig in his tent at Bir Hacheim, confident that his men's morale would survive the expected German onslaught

Above : French native troops man a light machine gun on an anti-aircraft mounting. *Below :* Last minute briefing before a French 'flying column' patrols into the German lines

Rommel strikes east

General de Larminat, Koenig's superior in the Western Desert

Rommel's offensive opened at dawn on 26th May with air attacks on the British airfields at Gambut and El Arid. In the afternoon, Gruppe Crüwell commenced its noisy demonstration against the front of the Gazala Line, assisted by elements of the main striking force, in an effort to mislead the British as to the direction of the coming assault. This deception plan had only limited success, for patrols from 7th Motor Brigade had already reported the massing of German armour around Rotonda Segnali. At 2030 hours the codeword Venezia crackled over German radio sets; *Panzerarmee Afrika* rolled forward into the night. 'Under magnificent moonlight', wrote Rommel, 'I set off with my staff at the head of the DAK for this armoured conflict. At times, in the distance, glows could be seen here and there . . . the Luftwaffe was trying to mark the position of Bir Hacheim with flares. Prey to extreme tension, I awaited the dawn with impatience. What would the enemy do? What had he already undertaken? Many questions ran through my head. Tomorrow would bring the answer. Ceaselessly, the surge of our engines pushed us forward . . .'

At Bir Hacheim, 26th May had begun much like any other day. General de Larminat, commander of Free French forces in the Western Desert, had visited the garrison on the previous day. A column, commanded by Major Amiel, was operating well forward, under the orders of 7th Motor Brigade. In the early afternoon Amiel reported the movement of large quantities of armour around Rotonda Segnali. As darkness fell, a flood of radio messages poured in, confirming Amiel's information. When the panzers began to advance, the French detachment fell back, with the columns of 7th Motor Brigade giving frequent situation reports. During the night, the splutter of engines and the characteristic squeaky rattle of tank tracks could be heard at Bir Hacheim as Rommel's armour churned its way through the desert to the south. In the north, the sky above the Gazala Line was lit up by parachute flares and flashes of gunfire.

At 0400 hours on 27th May elements of Amiel's patrol fell back within the perimeter, with the news that German light forces were just outside the southern edge of the minefield. Not long after this, the land lines to 7th Armoured Division and to the French rear echelon went dead. The reasons for this became apparent when signals personnel went out to check the wire, and were fired upon for their pains. At 0730 hours Koenig received a radio message from 7th Armoured Division announcing that battle had been joined, and that 4th Armoured Brigade was about to counterattack.

Things were going rather less well for the British than the hopeful tone of this message implied. Despite the fact that Rommel's concentration had been spotted and his advance shadowed, the German attack came as a rude surprise to some British formations. It is difficult to account for this depressing lack of preparedness; radio reports had been frequent and accurate, but little attention was paid to them. It has been suggested that 7th Armoured Division, a rather

Dawn 26th May. Rommel's great push against Gazala begins. A German 50mm anti-tank gun moves up, and a British 25-pounder goes into action

'The whole bloody Afrika Korps is drawn up in front of us like a bloody review' was the comment of one British officer. Rommel (below) kept close to the front of the German advance

patrician organisation, had a lofty disregard for any information not originating from its own sub-units.

Whatever the reason, 7th Armoured was caught dispersed and was roughly handled. The 3rd Indian Motor Brigade, in the desert south of Bir Hacheim, intimated cheerfully that 'the whole bloody Afrika Korps is drawn up in front of us like a bloody review'. The brigade was overrun at about 0630 hours, after a stiff but pitifully unequal fight. On the right flank of Rommel's advance, 90th Light swiftly overcame the elements of 7th Motor Brigade holding the Retma box. In the centre, 15th Panzer Division came upon 4th Armoured Brigade in process of deploying; the 4th Hussars were cut to pieces, and 3rd Royal Tank Regiment lost sixteen of its Grants. The panzers scythed on. HQ of 7th Armoured Division was overrun, and the divisional commander was captured temporarily. Major-General Lumsden ordered his 1st Armoured Division to the assistance of the 7th. But Lumsden's division, too, was unable to go into action as a concerted whole. The 22nd Armoured Brigade, five miles south of Naduret el Ghuesceuasc, tried to help, but was caught on the move by 15th and 21st Panzer Divisions, and was driven back towards Knightsbridge with the loss of thirty tanks.

During the afternoon the battle went less well for Rommel. The 2nd Armoured Brigade moved up from east of Knightsbridge, and took the German armour in the flank, while 1st Army Tank Brigade lumbered forward from north of Sidra ridge. Here Rommel suffered considerably; the 2nd Battalion of 104th Rifle Regiment was so badly crippled that it had to be disbanded and its survivors redistributed among the regiment's 1st and 3rd Battalions. There was a welter of confused, bitter fighting in the Knightsbridge area. At nightfall, the two German panzer divisions dug in between Rigel ridge and Bir Lefa, while the British armour leaguered

Advancing towards Bir Hacheim

for the night around 201st Guards Brigade in the Knightsbridge box. The supply echelons of the *Afrika Korps* had not managed to get further forward than Bir el Harmat; Rommel's panzers were thus marooned among the minefields and the British armour, and were running desperately short of petrol and ammunition. 90th Light and its accompanying reconnaissance units had chased off towards El Adem. Trieste and Ariete had reached Bir el Harmat only with difficulty; the former had made a serious navigational error during its approach march, and the latter had bloodied its knuckles against Bir Hacheim.

Koenig's brigade had stood-to since first light, awaiting attack. At about 0800 hours numerous vehicles appeared to the south of the position. There was, initially, some suspicion that this was 4th Armoured Brigade. This was soon dispelled as the vehicles swung round and moved forward in assault formation. As they drew

By nightfall on the first day Rommel's panzers had outrun their supply echelons and were thus marooned between the minefields and the British armour

closer, it could be seen that the tanks were the M 13/40s of Ariete. The first wave, consisting of about fifty tanks, crashed into the southern defences at 0900 hours. The Italian assault was delivered with commendable panache. Mines and anti-tank guns took a heavy toll, but six of the tanks managed to break into the position. These bore down upon a Legion company command post, where Captain Otte continued to give orders over the telephone until a tank appeared only fifteen yards away and put a shell through the top of his shelter. At this, Otte burnt his company's *fanion* to prevent its capture. His concern was premature. Some of the tanks were dealt with by the 75s firing at close range; the *Fusiliers-Marins*, too, joined in with their Bofors. The tough *légionnaires* disposed of the remainder, scrambling over them and firing revolvers through the observation slits.

A second attack, this time by thirty tanks, met with even less success. Shortly after 1000 hours the Italians withdrew. They had lost thirty-two tanks, no less than seven of which had been knocked out by a 75 crewed by *légionnaires*. Over sixty prisoners were taken, among them

the colonel commanding the Italian 132nd Armoured Regiment. This officer, although wounded, had changed from tank to tank three times as each was knocked out beneath him. Only one Frenchman had been wounded. Some useful supplies were extracted from the immobilised Italian vehicles, which appear to have been well-stocked with blankets, ham, preserves and eau-de-cologne. Ariete's assault, although delivered with determination, had been emphatically repulsed; Bir Hacheim was not attacked again that day. Some amusement was caused by the arrival, during the afternoon, of a message from the British colonel who was to have inspected the *Fusiliers-Marins* on their newly-learnt gun drill. The colonel regretted that, owing to the tactical situation, he would be unable to carry out the examination as planned.

There were several minor patrol actions on the night of 27th-28th May, and some more Italian prisoners were taken. During the morning of the 28th there was considerable air activity to the south, where planes of the RAF could be seen diving onto German columns. At about 1000 hours, Captain de Lamaze's detachment, covering the northern minefield, engaged some Italian armoured cars to the north-west. Two of these vehicles were hit by the 75s, and the remaining four made off into the minefield, where they promptly struck mines. In the afternoon, the Luftwaffe made the first of its all too frequent appearances. The *Bataillon du Pacifique* suffered badly from the bombing, but the *Fusiliers-Marins* demonstrated their skill on the Bofors by sending one of the attacking aircraft off trailing an ominous plume of smoke. A supply convoy came up during the night, bringing with it forty tons of much-needed 75mm ammunition. There was further skirmishes on the night of 28th-29th May, and still more Italians fell into French hands. Throughout the next day, the insistent roll of gunfire could be heard

away to the north, where the armoured battle raged round Knightsbridge.

Rommel continued to push northwards on the 28th. By nightfall on that day German troops had taken 'Commonwealth Keep', a small defensive post on the escarpment west of Acroma. Supplies of petrol and ammunition had dwindled alarmingly, though. Pavia and Trieste had failed to breach the minefield between Bir Hacheim and Sidi Muftah. A supply column – led in by Rommel himself – reached the isolated panzer divisions on the morning of 29th May, permitting Rommel to renew the battle. While 15th and 21st Panzer were refilling their vehicles, Crüwell ordered the Sabratha Division to attack the South Africans south of Gazala. This manoeuvre met with a warm reception; Sabratha ran into a tremendous artillery barrage, and fell back leaving 400 prisoners with Pienaar's men.

Rommel's tanks, meanwhile, had completed refuelling, and went into action against 2nd Armoured Brigade which, moving west from Knightsbridge, was trying to drive a wedge between the panzers and their support elements south of the Trigh Capuzzo. 22nd Armoured Brigade came up to help, but 4th Armoured Brigade (which still retained considerable fighting potential despite its mauling two days earlier) was not committed until the afternoon. Even then it was not used in the crucial tank battle, but was thrown against 90th Light around Bir el Harmat. This was another instance of British failure to concentrate armour to achieve a decisive result, and it was to have serious consequences. Both sides lost heavily, and the battle died at dusk.

The situation which faced Rommel was now uneviable. He was surrounded by inhospitable minefields and a

Top : A Krauss Maffi half-track
Centre : PzKw IIs move up
Bottom : A crashed Stuka south-west of Bir Hacheim

seemingly resolute, if a little disorganised, enemy. The failure of Pavia and Trieste to open the minefield meant that his line of supply ran round Bir Hacheim, and was subject to constant interference from the French. Some supplies, it is true, trickled through the minefield, but these were by no means adequate.

On the afternoon of 29th May Rommel received the cheerless news that Crüwell had been shot down while flying over the Gazala positions on a visit to X Corps. He was, it later transpired, captured by the British. Rommel's own Chief of Staff, General Gause, had been wounded, as had Colonel Westphal, his Chief of Operations. Fortunately for Rommel, Field-Marshal Kesselring happened to visit Crüwell's HQ shortly after the latter's disappearance. Von Mellenthin managed to persuade him to take over command of Crüwell's force for a few days, thus keeping control of the battle in German, rather than Italian, hands. The ener-getic and perceptive Colonel Bayerlein took over as Rommel's Chief of Staff. The infantry of X Corps had a measure of success in their mine-clearing attempts on the night of 29th-30th May. At the same time, Rommel decided to move into the area between Knightsbridge and Sidi Muftah, which has become known as the 'Cauldron'.

The discovery of the 150th Brigade box was an unpleasant surprise for Rommel, as his Intelligence had been unaware of its existence; he determined, though, to destroy the box and smash his way through the minefield to reopen his lines of supply. The narrow lane which the Italians had opened through the minefield was insufficient, and was under artillery fire from the Sidi Muftah box. If the *Afrika Korps* was to survive, it had to break out of the iron ring which encircled it. Rommel therefore concentrated all his efforts against 150th Brigade, leaving a screen of anti-

Rommel and Bayerlein (his Chief of Staff)

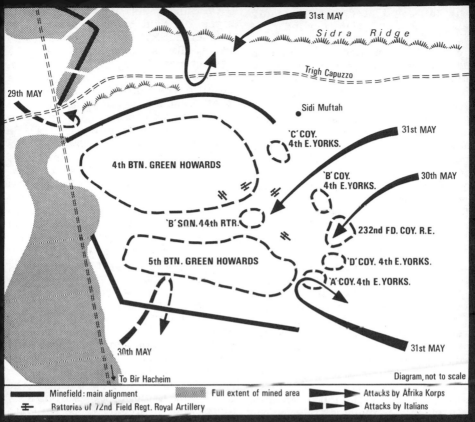

31st MAY

Sidra Ridge

Trigh Capuzzo

29th MAY

Sidi Muftah

'C' COY. 4th E. YORKS.

31st MAY

4th BTN. GREEN HOWARDS

'B' COY. 4th E. YORKS.

30th MAY

232nd FD. COY. R.E.

'B' SQN. 44th RTR.

5th BTN. GREEN HOWARDS

'D' COY. 4th E. YORKS.

'A' COY. 4th E. YORKS.

30th MAY

31st MAY

To Bir Hacheim

Diagram, not to scale

▬▬ Minefield : main alignment	▓▓ Full extent of mined area
╪ Batteries of 72nd Field Regt. Royal Artillery	

Attacks by Afrika Korps

Attacks by Italians

29th/31st May 1942. Rommel's attack on 150th Brigade in the Cauldron

tank guns, well laced with the deadly 88s, to hold off the remainder of Eighth Army.

While German armour massed in the Cauldron, things were relatively quiet at Bir Hacheim. Convoys passing within range of the position were shelled, and patrols went out at night to wreak havoc among the Axis supply echelons. Some enemy infiltration took place through the minefield to the north; Captain de Lamaze's detachment was heavily shelled and had to fall back temporarily within the main defensive perimeter. On 29th May a POW cage was set up for the growing number of Axis prisoners. With a flash of elegance, Koenig apologised to the captured officers for being unable to offer them more comfortable quarters. The following day patrols reported that the area immediately around Bir Hacheim was clear of the enemy. Vehicles could, however, be seen massing to the north-west, waiting to get through the minefield to resupply Rommel's armour in the Cauldron. Koenig stepped up his patrol activity, and sent a battery of 75s to join de Lamaze's detachment, in an effort to cover the northern minefield more closely.

At midday, there occurred an incident which might well have taxed the morale of a less eager formation. Six hundred Indian troops, mainly from 3rd Indian Motor Brigade, staggered into the position. They had been captured by the Germans, but later turned loose in the desert as their captors had neither food, water nor transport for them. The French fed these exhausted men, and made arrangements for their removal in one of the nightly supply convoys. The Indians gave the grim details of the destruction of their brigade, and added that four of their field guns still lay abandoned in the desert south-east of Bir Hachiem. A patrol of volunteers brought in three of these pieces. To the north, there was a warm engagement between de Lamaze and an enemy column.

On Sunday 31st May there were no signs of Axis activity around Bir Hacheim. XXX Corps HQ, which had repeatedly stressed to Koenig the importance of covering the minefield, expressed itself well pleased with the result of the fighting so far, but added that breaches in the minefield were still a major cause of concern. Lieutenant-Colonels Amilakvari and de Roux both led out motorised columns to harass enemy forces using these gaps. The former's patrol had considerable success, knocking out several tanks, but incurred a brisk counter-attack which caused numerous French casualties. A large supply convoy arrived on the night of 31st May-1st June, and with it came General de Larminat. He congratulated Koenig and his troops, and remarked particularly upon the garrison's tremendous morale. The convoy withdrew later the same night, taking with it the 600 Indians, 170 prisoners, and a number of French and Axis wounded. The convoy was shot at on its way out; several 88mm shells fell alarmingly close to the trucks which contained the prisoners. Radio messages from XXX Corps warned Koenig to be ready to advance. Accordingly, the rear echelon transport was concentrated at Bir bu Maafes, and the brigade prepared to move out.

Early on the morning of 1st June Koenig received the order to advance. A detailed movement order was set out in Koenig's Operational Order 11. The *Bataillon du Pacifique* was to lead the brigade forward, and Lieutenant-Colonel Broché's column, with artillery, anti-aircraft and anti-tank detachments accompanying it, left Bir Hacheim at 0900 hours. The remainder of the brigade was preparing to follow when an order came through from XXX Corps cancelling any further advance. Broché's column continued westwards, and, after knocking out one tank and shooting down four planes, reached El Telim by nightfall. Throughout the day, both the advancing battalion and the main position

Stukas, four of which were shot down by Koenig's *Fusiliers-Marins*, 1st June

were subjected to frequent air attacks. A dozen vehicles, including a water truck, a petrol tanker and an anti-aircraft truck, were destroyed.

Most frightening of the air raids were the dive-bombing attacks of the Stukas. These planes screamed down on the position, dropped bombs which sent fountains of sand into the air, and roared off. The *Fusiliers-Marins* manned their Bofors with determination, shooting down four Stukas on 1st June. The Bofors consumed ammunition at an extravagant rate, but 1,000 rounds arrived with the supply column on the night of 1st-2nd June, and more was promised. Koenig decided not to unload the supplies from the vehicles which had brought them up. An advance still seemed probable, so he kept the vehicles at hand, sending them to bivouac a mile to the north, to minimise the danger from air attack.

On the morning of 2nd June, Koenig considered visiting HQ 7th Armoured Division, to obtain up-to-date information on the state of the battle. At the last minute, he decided to remain at Bir Hacheim, and sent Captain Tomkins to 7th Armoured in-

stead. Koenig's decision proved to be a wise one; Tomkins fell in with a German patrol and was captured. There was little news of the progress of Broché's column. The colonel's radio functioned badly; this was doubly frustrating, since all other radio links were working perfectly. Messages from Broché were hopelessly garbled, and the column could be contacted only with difficulty.

Not long after dawn, de Lamaze reported numerous vehicles to the north. Koenig asked the captain if he was certain that the vehicles were hostile. There was some hesitation, followed by the dry comment that there were fifty tanks and one hundred other vehicles in sight, and some of these were already firing on the detachment. A frantic message was sent to the convoy bivouacked outside the perimeter, and the trucks scuttled in pursued by shell bursts. At this time in the morning there was usually a thick mist wreathing the position, and 2nd June was no exception. Under cover of this mist, a detachment of *Infanterie de la Marine* under Captain Laborde, together with the 22nd North African Company and a battery of 75s, moved into the sector vacated by the *Bataillon du Pacifique*. The anticipated attack

113

failed to materialise. Instead, two Italian officers presented themselves at the outposts of the Legion under a flag of truce. Captain de Sairigne conducted the Italians, blindfolded, to Koenig's command post. Here the two officers saluted, and the senior began an oration in Italian. The value of this discourse was rather limited by the fact that neither Koenig nor Lieutenant-Colonel Masson, his Chief of Staff, spoke Italian. Nevertheless, the gist of the message seemed to be that the Axis command advised surrender to avoid a useless effusion of blood.

'Gentlemen', replied Koenig, 'thank your generals for their pleasant conduct, but tell them that there is no question of surrender'. The Italians endeavoured, without success, to persuade the French general to change his mind. They were led back to the perimeter, and returned to their own lines. Following the retirement of the Italian emissaries, Koenig sent out a radio message ordering the *Bataillon du Pacifique* to return; he also ordered de Lamaze to 'come back immediately, there's work for you'. A further message was sent to the brigade's rear echelon at Bir bu Maafes, forbidding it to move forward. The French general warned his unit commanders that assault was imminent. 'General Rommel', said Koenig, 'has asked us to surrender and has threatened us with extermination. I have refused. Do your duty'. There followed instructions on the conduct of the defensive battle. 'In the case of breakthrough by enemy tanks into the infantry positions', ordered Koenig, 'remain at your posts and fight the enemy infantry.'

Throughout the afternoon an increasing weight of shells fell on Bir Hacheim, though the 75s of the 1st Artillery replied where possible. The artillery duel was interrupted by a sudden sandstorm, and as darkness fell the firing died away. Early the following morning the *Bataillon du Pacifique*, having sustained some losses on its journey, returned to Bir

Hacheim and took up its former sector of the perimeter. As the sun rose to bring another scorching day, the heavy crash of German 105mm field guns announced to the defenders that the battle for Bir Hacheim had reached a new, more serious, phase.

The garrison of Bir Hacheim had little idea of the magnitude of the conflict that rolled across the desert to their north. Having concentrated his armour behind a ring of anti-tank guns on 30th May, Rommel fell on 150th Brigade in the Sidi Muftah box. Brigadier C W Haydon's command included 4th Battalion, the East Yorkshire Regiment, 4th and 5th Battalions, the Green Howards, and 72nd Field Regiment, Royal Artillery, with the Matildas of 44th Royal Tank Regiment in support. 150th Brigade held out bravely under the sledgehammer blows of Rommel's armour. The Germans were becoming increasingly desperate. When a captured British officer complained to Rommel of the paucity of the water issued to the prisoners, the German general replied; 'You are getting exactly the same ration of water as the *Afrika Korps* and myself – half a cup. But I agree that we cannot go on like this. If we don't get a convoy through tonight, I shall have to ask General Ritchie for terms.' Ritchie, regrettably, seemed unaware of the parlous plight of his adversary. The men of 150th Brigade fought on unsupported.

On 1st June the panzers finally broke in, and the last unit of the brigade surrendered at about 1430 hours. The fall of Sidi Muftah freed Rommel from his immediate crisis. Ritchie signalled to Auchinleck that he was 'much distressed' by this defeat, but nevertheless considered that the situation was improving. Auchinleck replied that he viewed 'the consolidation of a broad and deep wedge in the middle of your position with some misgiving', and urged Ritchie to move onto the offensive. Several opportunities for a British counterattack presented themselves.

The effect of the Stukas' attacks on No-Man's Land near Bir Hacheim

A thrust could be made down the Via Balbia, towards Tmimi though this would give Rommel a free hand for an advance from the Cauldron. Another possibility – and a very exciting one – was for XIII Corps to attack the Cauldron from the north, while XXX Corps swept around Bir Hacheim, and then swung north to take the *Afrika Korps* in the rear. A third, less enterprising, plan, would simply involve a frontal assault on Rommel's positions in the Cauldron. The latter scheme was eventually adopted, though its formulation was confused and its employment uninspired. While XIII Corps attacked Sidra ridge on the northern lip of the Cauldron, XXX was to move against Aslagh ridge, on the eastern side.

The attack did not get off the ground till 5th June, and both prongs of the assault were speedily blunted. This is hardly surprising. One of the formations involved, 5th Indian Division, had recently arrived from Iraq, and had been held as army reserve during the earlier stages of the battle. Ariete was pushed off Aslagh ridge, but 9th Indian Infantry Brigade and 22nd Armoured Brigade could get no further forward than this. Only when the eastern attack had bogged down in a sea of bursting shells and burning tanks, did 32nd Army Tank Brigade lurch forward against 21st Panzer Division on Sidra ridge. This attack was put in with great determination, but insufficient artillery support; 32nd Army Tank Brigade lost fifty tanks out of the seventy engaged. In the afternoon, leading the battle with his usual finesse, Rommel riposted. 21st Panzer ripped south-eastwards to Bir el Tamar, while 15th Panzer exploited a gap in the minefield near Bir el Harmat, and poured over Aslagh ridge. 10th Indian Infantry Brigade was surrounded on the ridge, and waited for support which never came. On 6th June, while the Mark IIIs of

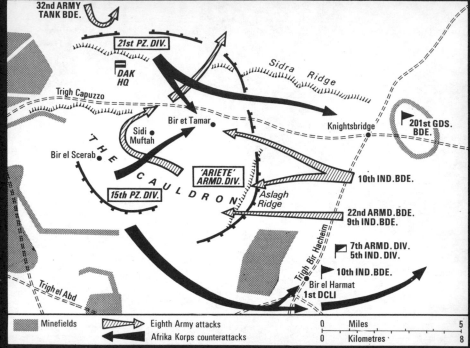

32nd ARMY TANK BDE.

21st PZ. DIV.

DAK HQ

Sidra Ridge

Trigh Capuzzo

Bir et Tamar

Knightsbridge

201st GDS. BDE.

Sidi Muftah

Bir el Scerab

T H E C A U L D R O N

'ARIETE' ARMD. DIV.

15th PZ. DIV.

Aslagh Ridge

10th IND. BDE.

22nd ARMD. BDE.
9th IND. BDE.

7th ARMD. DIV.
5th IND. DIV.

10th IND. BDE.

Trigh Bir Hacheim

Bir el Harmat

1st DCLI

Trigh el Abd

| Minefields | Eighth Army attacks | 0 | Miles | 5 |
| Afrika Korps counterattacks | | 0 | Kilometres | 8 |

5th/6th June 1942. The frontal assault on Rommel's positions in the Cauldron

15th Panzer lacerated the Indians on Aslagh ridge, the British armour milled about, beset by contradictory orders. The Indians and four regiments of field artillery on the ridge continued to defend themselves with hopeless valour. The gunners fought their 25-pounders to the last. An Italian officer witnessed one troop of guns remaining in action until only one man was left; this individual then fired each gun in turn, and continued to do so until he was shot down. A British artillery officer who visited the battlefield as the tide of war swept past it again some six months later, found the guns still in position and the bodies of their crews sprawled in the sand beside them. On this terrible day 10th Indian Infantry Brigade, the support group of 22nd Armoured Brigade, and four regiments of field artillery, were almost totally destroyed. Other formations sustained heavy punishment; in all, Eighth Army lost 6,000 men and about 150 tanks. Ritchie's counterattack, so long in gestation, had aborted in the most grisly fashion. Having thus disposed, in no uncertain fashion, of the threat to the Cauldron, Rommel prepared to deal at his leisure with that thorn in his flank, Bir Hacheim.

While British hopes vanished in the dust and smoke of the Cauldron, the garrison of Bir Hacheim was subjected to air attacks of increasing ferocity. German sources state that 1,300 sorties were flown against Bir Hacheim between 2nd–9th June. Some of the sting was taken out of the Luftwaffe by the planes of the Desert Air Force, which managed to intercept several of the German attacks. 2nd June was particularly successful. 'Bravo', signalled Koenig to Air Vice-Marshal Coningham, 'Merci pour la RAF.' 'Merci pour le sport', was Coningham's reply. In the desert war in general, the air element was of pivotal importance. At Bir Hacheim, however, the effectiveness of German air power was limited by several factors. Firstly, the garrison was largely infantry, and therefore did not offer an easily-observed target as did, for example, a tank. There were, it is true, a large number of lorries on and around the position, but these were widely dispersed and in some cases dug in. The excellence of French defences was a decisive limitation on the effect of bombs and shells. Rommel himself gave a balanced judgement on the value of the defences. He noted the 'skilfully prepared field positions and strong points, slit trenches, light machine gun and anti-tank gun positions, dotted all over the terrain, with each separate strong-point surrounded by a strong mine belt . . . this kind of fortification is practically proof against artillery fire and air attacks, as all a direct hit can do is destroy one small slit trench or so. A very high expenditure of ammunition is necessary to inflict real damage.'

From daybreak on 3rd June the attack on Bir Hacheim gained momentum. The artillery duel began at first light, but, to the chagrin of the French artillerymen, their 75s were unable to reach the German 105s which were hammering away at the position. During the morning, two Englishmen appeared outside the perimeter. One of them was the driver of the unfortunate Captain Tomkins, captured on the previous day. He carried a message from Rommel, scribbled on a page from a German signals pad.

'To the troops at Bir Hakim [sic]. Any further resistance will only serve to shed more useless blood. You will suffer the same fate as the two British brigades which were exterminated at Got el Ualeb two days ago.

'We shall cease fire when you raise the white flag and come towards us without arms. Signed: Rommel.'

Koenig made no reply to Rommel's ultimatum. Instead, he sent an order to his unit commanders, assessing the situation and giving his instructions. '1. Soon we must expect a large-scale attack. The enemy will employ aeroplanes, tanks, artillery and infantry. 2. It is my order and wish that every

man will do his duty unflinchingly, either at his post or isolated from his comrades.

3. Our task is to hold the ground, whatever the cost, until our victory is complete.

4. This order must be clearly conveyed to all ranks.

5. Good luck to you all.'

In an effort to crack the morale of the garrison, Rommel called in the Stukas. In the two hours between 1130 hours and 1330 hours there were four separate attacks, each delivered by a swarm of planes. A grave shortage of 40mm ammunition for the Bofors guns restricted the French reply to these raids. RAF support was extremely effective. One group of twelve Stukas arrived over the position at the same time as a patrol of Hurricanes. Seven of the dive-bombers were shot down, and the British planes flew off accompanied by wild cheers from the troops below.

Although the pace of the bombardment did not slacken, there were no serious ground attacks on Bir Hacheim during the first few days of June. Elements of 90th Light and Trieste were in position around Bir Hacheim, but were unable to give it their full attention due to fierce British patrol activity. Harassed though the British High Command was, it still found time to organise ground support for the French. Particular credit is due to Brigadier Renton's 7th Motor Brigade, whose columns struck well into the German rear. The men who drove in the supply convoys, night after night, also deserve special mention. They had to operate in country alive with German patrols, and find their way into Bir Hacheim through the minefields that ringed it. Yet without their efforts, Bir Hacheim might, despite the valour of its defenders, have gone the same way as the Sidi Muftah box, whose resistance was hampered by lack of water and ammunition.

Koenig sends out patrols when he is ordered to advance on 1st June

On Thursday, 4th June, the artillery and air bombardment continued. As the 75s had fired 2,500 rounds the previous day, and had only 500 left, they made only occasional replies to the hostile artillery. A radio message from Eighth Army promised that more ammunition would be sent in as soon as possible, and informed Koenig that a British counteroffensive – the ill-omened Operation Aberdeen against the Cauldron – would be launched next day. At 0430 hours on 5th June the Germans made yet another effort to persuade the garrison to lay down its arms. A German officer in a truck drove up to the positions held by the 5th Company of the 2nd Battalion of the Legion, and demanded a parley. The Legion sentry happened to be a German, and he told the officer, in no uncertain terms, that Koenig had forbidden any negotiation. The officer drove off in high dudgeon, but had only gone a few yards when his vehicle hit a mine and stopped in a cloud of smoke. The officer and his driver leapt out, and continued on foot.

During the night the garrison had been resupplied with water and ammunition. There was now sufficient water to give two litres a day for each man for three days, with another three day's supply in reserve. Six thousand rounds of ammunition for the 75s had also come up, and the artillery was able to reopen its counterbattery shoots. Unfortunately, the Germans were now using some 155mm guns, which well outranged the 75s. The French artillery made an effort to reach these pieces by moving outside the perimeter, and at least prevented the German batteries from closing in. Later in the day, German infantry made some attempts at infiltration, but were stopped 1,500 yards away by the 75s and mortars. German casualties were heavy; Colonel Wolz's combat group, consisting of light flak units backed by the panzergrenadiers of 90th Light, was badly shot up and failed to gain much ground.

Above and below : A French 75mm in action at Bir Hacheim, and a British 25-pounder at 'Knightsbridge'. *Right :* Rommel plans the next move

On 6th June, the day on which Rommel broke out of the Cauldron, the situation worsened at Bir Hacheim. Two powerful attacks by infantry with tank support went in against the *Bataillon du Pacifique*, which beat off both assaults but incurred numerous casualties in doing so. To the west, about twenty tanks appeared outside the minefield and fired into the position. The artillery replied vigorously, but was handicapped by a shortage of ammunition; the guns were reduced to firing one round per minute, and later, only one gun in each battery was allowed to fire. Sunday, 7th June was a relatively quiet day. The bombardment died down somewhat, and there was only one Stuka raid. The surveillance group to the north was finally ejected from its position by a determined attack, and fell back, this time permanently, into the main perimeter. After dark, a much-needed munitions convoy arrived; fifteen vehicles, including two water trucks with 2,000 litres of water, rumbled into the French lines.

8th June dawned with thick fog surrounding the position, blinding French observation posts. Behind the blanket of fog the French could hear the rattle of tank tracks and the shouts of infantry deploying for the attack. Rommel had at last decided to eliminate Bir Hacheim, and had sent a strong detachment of 15th Panzer to assist 90th Light and Trieste. As the fog cleared, German artillery opened up with sharp ferocity, concentrating on the *Bataillon de Marche*. Stukas screamed down on the defences, and fighters swept over the desert, machine-gunning observation posts and battery positions.

At 1055 hours the panzergrenadiers of 15th Panzer, well supported by tanks and light armour, advanced against the north-western sector. The German infantry pressed forward with enthusiasm; Point 186, an important piece of comparatively high ground, seemed to be their objective. The *Bataillon de Marche* gave a good account of itself, but was forced back, losing men rapidly. Its 6th Company was decimated, and had to be reinforced by the 22nd North African Company. The Bren carriers of the Legion stood by to rush men into the threatened sector in the event of a breakthrough. Sixty Stukas delivered an attack in the early afternoon, inflicting still

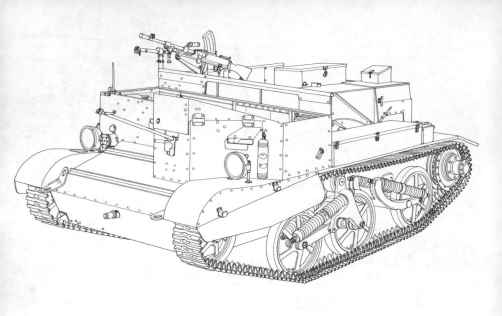

The British Universal Carrier, more commonly (and incorrectly) called the Bren Gun Carrier, was a standardised version of the various models of its predecessor, the Carrier, of which the Bren Carrier was correctly one. About 35,000 Universal Carriers were built during the war, and served in all the theatres where British troops served. They fulfilled roles ranging from gun towing to infantry transport, via mortar platforms. *Weight:* 3.95 tons. *Crew:* 4/5. *Speed:* 32mph. *Range:* 160 miles. *Engine:* Ford petrol engine, 85hp. *Length:* 12 feet 4 inches. *Width:* 6 feet 11 inches. *Height:* 5 feet 3 inches. *Armament:* one .303-inch Bren light machine gun and/or one .5-inch Boys antitank rifle. *Armour:* 12mm

more damage upon the hard-pressed garrison. The German infantry loped forward again even before the dust of the Stuka's bombs had settled. The artillery observation post at Point 186 had been silent since just before midday, and the fire of the 75s suffered as a result. Another wave of infantry swarmed forward, this time against the Legion's sector. The entire northern front was under heavy attack. The lines to Koenig's command post were cut by shellfire, and dust and smoke obscured the general's view of the battle. The situation became increasingly grave. Many of the anti-tank guns were knocked out; one 75 sustained a direct hit, and was blown to pieces together with its crew. A chance German shell hit one of the

ammunition dumps, which exploded with a flash and a roar.

Koenig sent out renewed orders to his unit commanders, stressing that the infantry were to stay put even if overrun by armour. They must, Koenig urged, let the tanks pass over them, and then rise to deal with the infantry who would be following up. All artillery pieces were to concentrate on stopping the tanks. Finally, ordered Koenig, if capture was imminent, all secret documents were to be burnt. As night fell, the circle of defenders remained unbroken – though badly bent. The *Battaillon de Marche* in the north-west had lost a good deal of ground; the battalion's 6th Company had been withdrawn into brigade reserve, and its place in the line taken by the 22nd North African Company. Medical arrangements were on the verge of breaking down. The brigade's medical staff were grossly overloaded, and strove, under hideous conditions, to treat the growing numbers of wounded. The general shortage of water meant that there was little available for washing wounds. Plasma, sulfonamide and anaesthetics were also dangerously low. The RAF managed to drop some medical supplies on8th June, but the parachute failed to open and the vital container plummeted into the ground, shattering its contents.

In spite of the extreme seriousness of the situation facing the garrison, morale remained buoyant. There was a widespread realisation that the issue at stake was a much broader one than simply the fate of a cross tracks in the middle of a featureless desert. There was more, much more, to it than that. True, if Bir Hacheim fell, Rommel would be able to turn on the remainder of Eighth Army, still groggy after its defeat in the Cauldron. Yet the real issue was deeper still. If Koenig's men failed to do all that could be expected of them, then the death-knell of the French army would have tolled for the second time in two years. Obviously, after several days' hard fighting, and with the prospect of more to come, the defenders of Bir Hacheim did not romanticise their rôle. Thirst, pain, wounds and death were all they could expect. They were, nevertheless, determined to hold on. The Free French in all parts of the world watched the progress of the battle with pride intermingled with concern. De Gaulle, broadcasting from London, congratulated the beleaguered garrison. 'General Koenig,' he said, 'know, and tell your troops, that the whole of France is looking at you, and you are her pride.' A message of Koenig's, sent to Eighth Army on the evening of 8th June, summed up the garrison's resolve. 'We are surrounded.' 'Our thoughts are always near you. We have

confidence. Long live Free France.'

Tuesday, 9th June, was another blistering desert day. The garrison was by now very tired; their sleep was constantly interrupted by night alarms, and by German flares which bathed Bir Hacheim in their ghostly light. Their water, rations and ammunition were running low, but with thin, stubbly faces, they peered into the dawn mist and steeled themselves to meet the next attack. As a prelude, German guns and aircraft drenched the position in a wave of high explosive. The telephone wires between the observation and command posts and the artillery positions were cut yet again – and there was no longer any wire left with which to renew them. At 1300 hours the attack developed, against the *Bataillon du Pacifique* and the *Bataillon de Marche*. The advancing German infantry were aided by tanks and 50mm guns which moved up in close support and knocked out still more of the 75s. The Germans fought their way forward doggedly, and managed to drive a wedge between two companies of the *Bataillon de Marche*. There was a whirl of ugly hand-to-hand fighting; one German soldier was shot down only a few yards from a 75. For a moment it seemed as if the African troops would crumble under the tremendous pressure. When collapse seemed inevitable, there was a roar and clatter from the rear as one of the Legion's Bren carrier sections rushed up. The *légionnaires* were relatively fresh, and they plugged the gap, forcing back the enemy infantry.

In the south, too, the garrison was under heavy attack. Elements of 90th Light, whose artillery had been supporting the attack in the north, swung round and assaulted the *Bataillon du Pacifique*. The Germans suffered badly – 250 bodies were counted in front of the battalion's positions – but by nightfall they had established themselves just over 200 yards from the fort. These attacks were accompanied by more subtle

Without shirt, but with greatcoat,
a bearded French soldier

attempts to bring about the fall of Bir Hacheim. A radio message, allegedly from 7th Armoured Division, reached Koenig's command post. 'We are ourselves attacked', it announced despondently, 'and cannot help you. Tell your chief to surrender to avoid further bloodshed.' The message was delivered in halting English, with traces of a German accent, and fooled nobody. At 2000 hours a massive Stuka attack pounded the encircled position. One bomb fell on a dressing-station, killing nineteen of the wounded. Several lorries were hit, and most of the unissued rations destroyed. The *Bataillon du Pacifique* suffered a grievous blow; Lieutenant-Colonel Broché and his adjutant, Captain de Bricourt, were both killed when a shell hit the battalion command post. The attackers also sustained heavy casualties; a combat group under Colonel Hecker, commander of the *Panzerarmee*'s engineers, had been spearheading the assault since the evening of 8th June, and had lost ten of its eleven tanks, and much of its infantry. Hecker was reinforced by *Gruppe* Baade, two battalions of 115th Panzer Grenadier Regiment, from 15th Panzer Division. Baade's men were also badly mauled, particularly in the bitter fighting around the old fort at the southern end of the position.

By dusk on 9th June it was obvious to Koenig that Bir Hacheim could not be held much longer. Point 186 had been lost, and the Germans were now able to dominate the *Bataillon de Marche*'s sector. The situation in the south, around the fort, was also crucial. Losses of both men and equipment had been high, and the omnipresent ammunition shortage was a constant source of concern. Koenig was confronted by the decision of whether to remain at Bir Hacheim and incur almost certain annihilation in the near future, or to attempt to break out. Ritchie had constantly urged Koenig to hold on, but on the afternoon of 9th June 7th Armoured

Division asked Koenig, over the radio, if he deemed it advisable to pull out. Koenig replied that he was in favour of a breakout, providing he could be provided with sufficient transport in which to get his wounded away. As 7th Armoured was unable to produce sufficient vehicles on the night of 9th–10th June, it was decided that the breakout should occur on the following night.

On 10th June Colonel Baade's combat group made considerable progress in the north, breaking into the main defensive line. Lieutenant Dewey's Bren carrier section roared forward to counterattack, and a fierce fight ensued. Rommel himself was present with *Gruppe* Baade at the time, and commented on the ferocity of the combat, 'with the French desperately defending every single nest of resistance and suffering terrible casualties as a result'. By a supreme effort, Dewey's *légionnaires* succeeded in containing the breakin. One particularly nasty feature of 10th June was a large-scale air raid in mid-morning, in which 110 aircraft attacked the position. No less than 130 tons of bombs fell on Bir Hacheim during the course of the day. That night Rommel reported to his High Command in Germany that he was confident of taking Bir Hacheim next day. This came, no doubt, none too soon for Kesselring, who had viewed the Luftwaffe's losses over the position with growing dismay. He had already urged Rommel to overrun the French with tanks, so as to conserve the air arm; Rommel correctly realised, though, that a massed tank attack on Bir Hacheim could result only in very heavy tank losses in the minefields. By the evening of 10th June Rommel was convinced, then, that one more major effort would result in the collapse of the French. He was probably not far from wrong. During 10th June, the garrison's mortars had fired the last of their ammunition, and the field guns had only a few more rounds remaining. As the Germans prepared for what must have been the decisive assault, Koenig planned his breakout.

Withdrawal is undoubtedly the most difficult phase of war. It is almost always performed at a time when morale is shaky; it requires meticulous planning and a carefully considered timetable. A minor mistake can produce not merely a slight tactical reverse, but a major disaster. Night is the ideal time at which to withdraw, though darkness adds greatly to the problems of control and navigation. The hazards confronting the French in their breakout from Bir Hacheim were numerous. Koenig had to extract a large force, with transport and equipment, from the position, and bring it safely through the minefields, past a vigilant enemy. The most obvious route out was to the east, through the Legion's positions. Koenig decided not to use this path, however, as it would seem to the Germans his most probable line of withdrawal. Instead, he gave orders for a passage 150 yards wide to be opened in the western minefield, just north of the old fort. The reliable 7th Motor Brigade undertook to provide a convoy of lorries and ambulances in the desert about five miles south-west of Bir Hacheim, and Koenig proposed to effect a junction with this force. A detailed operations order laid down the full plan for the breakout. Units in contact with the enemy were to be left behind till the last possible moment; two companies were to remain behind as a deception party. Any equipment that could not be taken out was to be destroyed. All secret documents were put in Koenig's command vehicle, with the exception of a few of the most important, which were kept in Lieutenant-Colonel Masson's briefcase.

As is the case with so many military operations, things did not go according to plan. It took longer to load the vehicles than had been expected, and communication between Koenig and his unit commanders, and these officers and their sub-units, was

difficult. At 2030 hours the leading element, the medical convoy, began to move out. It was followed by the *Bataillon du Pacifique* and the *Bataillon de Marche*. The *Fusiliers-Marins* seem to have had problems with their night navigation. One of their guns, together with its towing vehicle, fell into a large hole and had to be left behind. The German artillery contributed to the growing chaos by opening up, setting fire to several vehicles whose flames lit up the position. The remainder of the breakout was a nightmare. Shells were bursting on the abandoned defences, and parachute flares drifted over the arid landscape. There was sustained machine gun fire from both flanks, and confused struggles with groups of German infantry. Cadet Officer Bellec, who was responsible for navigating the HQ column, ran into a minefield. He made two more attempts, but was blown up on each occasion. Koenig ordered his party to swing to the south to avoid the mines, and at about 0300 hours he caught up with the main body of the brigade, which was held up by stiff German opposition. Koenig ordered Captain de Lamaze to clear a path for the column; there was a grim engagement in which de Lamaze and the redoubtable Lieutenant Dewey were killed. Several vehicles were set on fire, but the brigade managed to resume its advance, though cohesion had been utterly lost and it was impossible to regroup. Nevertheless, most of the garrison managed, somehow or other, to reach the rendezvous with 7th Motor Brigade.

Initially, it seemed as if casualties had been very heavy. At 0700 hours on the 11th, both Koenig and Amilakvari were missing, and under 1,500 troops had reached British lines. The picture steadily improved as the day progressed. At 0800 hours 7th Motor Brigade signalled that 2,000 French soldiers were safely through. Four hours later, Koenig and Amilakvari reached Gasr el Arid, and the latter

A shattered PzKw, towed to a road-side dumping ground near Bir Hacheim

set about regrouping the Legion on the Trigh Capuzzo. By nightfall there were 2,500 Frenchmen at Gasr el Arid, and still more were helped in during the night and the following day by the columns of 7th Motor Brigade.

The French withdrawal from Bir Hacheim had, in fact, proved a remarkable success. Rommel noted with irritation that 'in spite of all our security measures, the greater part of the garrison broke out . . . under the leadership of their commander, General Koenig.' The German general blamed his failure to intercept the withdrawal on the fact that the task of sealing off the fortress was not properly carried out. It seems more than probable, though, that Rommel's efficient wireless intercept service had obtained accurate information as to the time of the operation; this makes German failure all the more difficult to understand. On the morning of 11th June 90th Light at last occupied Bir Hacheim. 'Some 500 French soldiers', wrote Rommel, 'fell into our hands, the majority of them wounded.' Bayerlein examined the position closely, and discovered, to his amazement, over 1,200 separate nests for infantry and heavy weapons.

French casualties totalled 900, two-thirds of which were sustained during the course of the evacuation. A good deal of equipment had been lost. Forty of the 75s did not return; twenty-four of these were lost in the breakout, and the others were damaged or destroyed while in position. Much of the brigade's transport had also been destroyed. But if French losses had been high, so too had those of the Axis forces. Fifty-one tanks, five self-propelled guns, fifteen armoured cars and seven planes were disposed of by the garrison of Bir Hacheim. Numerous German and Italian infantry, too, had been killed and wounded by French fire. It must be emphasised that casualty figures, for both sides, cannot be regarded as definitive. The *section historique* of the French army gives substantially higher French casualty figures; forty-four officers were killed or wounded in the actual fighting, and 1,104 soldiers were likewise killed or wounded during the same period. Losses during the breakout were 130 killed, 198 wounded and 829 missing. These figures strike the author as being somewhat too high; they also conflict with several other sources. The discrepancy may well be explained by the fact that the *section historique*'s figures include walking wounded, whereas other sources apparently do not. Axis losses, too, are subject to the same sort of fluctuation; furthermore, it is difficult to establish when an armoured vehicle is totally destroyed, and when it is wholly or partially recoverable.

The defence of Bir Hacheim bought time for Eighth Army. Rommel was not ready to resume his operations until the afternoon of 11th June. While 21st Panzer Division held Sidra ridge, 15th Panzer pushed on to Naduret el Ghesceuasc, with 90th Light swinging round south of the El Adem box. On 12th June 15th Panzer received orders to remain on the defensive, as 21st Panzer moved south of Knightsbridge to take the British armour facing 15th Panzer in the flank. Due to British hesitation – largely as a result of a disagreement between General Messervy and his brigadiers – the expected attacks against 15th Panzer failed to materialise, and General Nehring ordered the division forward. At midday 21st Panzer also attacked. In a confused day's fighting, the British lost over 100 tanks, and with them the last chance of winning the Gazala battles.

Ritchie had, for some days, been in favour of a withdrawal to the Egyptian frontier, but both Churchill and Auchinleck were firmly opposed to such a manoeuvre. The latter urged Ritchie to form a new line from Bir el Gubi, through El Adem, to Acroma and the coast. 'Tobruk must be held', urged Auchinleck, 'and the enemy must not be allowed to invest it.' Ritchie unwisely agreed to take up this new line, but failed to emphasise to either Cairo or London the very battered condition of Eighth Army. 201st Guards Brigade broke out from Knightsbridge on the night of 13th-14th June. There remained the problem of 1st South African Division and 50th Division, still holding the northern portion of the outflanked Gazala Line. General Pienaar skillfully extracted his division on 14th-15th June. For General Ramsden's Northumbrians the task was less easy. 59th Division had already lost one of its brigades, and was encircled by hostile forces. The only point in Ramsden's favour was that he had a a plentiful supply of transport, petrol, and ammunition. Ramsden and his staff arrived at a decision which was enterprising, if risky. The division would break out to the west, and then turn south, round Bir Hacheim, before heading

8th June. Rommel decides to eliminate Bir Hacheim. Artillery opens up,
Stukas scream down and the panzers advance as the dawn fog clears. Koenig
sent a message to Eighth Army : 'We have confidence. Long live Free France'

Further north, the British were forced to fall back, and all depended
on the French force. De Gaulle broadcast : 'know, and tell your troops,
that the whole of France is looking at you, and you are her pride'

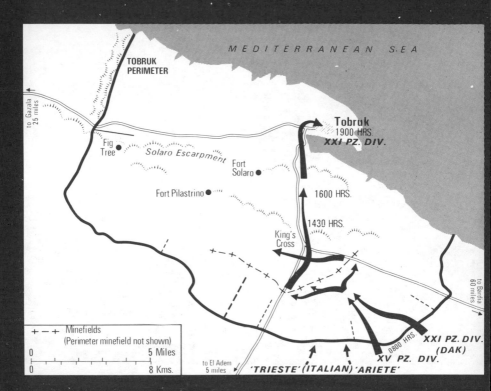

20th June 1942. Rommel takes Tobruk

Above : By 10th June the French had run out of ammunition and were forced to evacuate Bir Hacheim. *Below :* Koenig had bought time for Eighth Army, but not enough, for by the 21st Rommel had taken Tobruk. Twenty-four hours later he was on the Egyptian frontier again

east. In the event, Ramsden's plan proved totally successful, and the greater part of his division got clean away. The escape of 1st South African and 50th Divisions were the only glimmers of hope in a picture of otherwise unrelieved gloom.

Ritchie soon realised that the El Adem-Acroma line was untenable, and decided instead to hold Tobruk with XIII Corps, with the wreckage of XXX Corps covering its desert flank. 'Fortress Tobruk' itself was entrusted to Major-General Klopper of 2nd South African Division. 32nd Army Tank Brigade, 201st Guards Brigade and 11th Indian Infantry Brigade, with the South Africans, made up the garrison. Prospects for a sustained defence were bleak. The defence of the 'fortress' had fallen into disrepair; air support was weak, and no help could be offered by the navy. While 29th Indian Infantry Brigade held out in the El Adem box, commanding Axis By-pass, there was still hope. But the Indians withdrew on the night of 16th–17th June and, in von Mellenthin's words, 'from that moment on the defence of Tobruk ceased to be a serious operation of war'.

By 18th June Rommel had surrounded Tobruk. The *Afrika Korps* and Ariete concentrated around Gambut, and moved up to the perimeter on the night of 19th–20th June; at dawn on the 20th the storm broke. Stukas swooped malevolently ahead of the armour. Though the defenders fought hard, they were grievously short of anti-tank weapons and could make little impression on the thrusting mailed fist of Rommel's armour. XXX Corps tried to counterattack towards Sidi Rezegh, but was easily held off by 90th Light. The outer

defences of Tobruk were soon pierced, and Klopper lacked the means to restore the situation. In the afternoon, German tanks swept into Tobruk town, beneath a pall of smoke from burning supply dumps. Klopper was unable to obtain permission to break out during the night, and, shortly after dawn on 21st June, surrendered with most of the 33,000 troops under his command. Rommel did not spend long savouring his victory. At 0945 hours he signalled laconically 'Fortress Tobruk has capitulated. All units will reassemble and prepare for further advance.' Twenty-four hours later, Rommel was on the Egyptian frontier, having won the most remarkable victory of his career, and having inflicted on Eighth Army a defeat which shook it to the core.

The German advance surged in past Tobruk, and halted only at El Alamein. This was to prove the highwater mark of Axis success, and it was from the Alamein position that the revitalised Eighth Army, under the command of General Montgomery, counter-attacked in October 1942. Prospects for such a move seemed, however, very distant indeed as Eighth Army fell back eastwards at the end of June. German radio was exultant over the outcome of the Gazala battles. The fall of Bir Hacheim was made much of in Axis propaganda.

On 12th June the Germans announced that they had 'stormed Bir Hacheim' and went on to announce grimly that 'the white and coloured Frenchmen taken at Bir Hacheim, since they do not belong to a regular army . . . will be executed.' De Gaulle instantly made a counterthreat. The BBC warned the Germans that 'if the German army were so far to dishonour itself as to kill French soldiers taken prisoner when fighting for their country, General de Gaulle announces that, to his profound regret, he would find himself obliged to inflict the same fate on the German prisoners who

**Tobruk yielded 33,000 prisoners ;
Eighth Army was shaken to its core**

Rommel takes a little light refreshment in Tobruk after having won the most remarkable victory of his career

The German advance halts at El Alamein, from where (four months later) a revitalised Eighth Army counterattacked under Montgomery

have fallen into the hands of his troops.' This threat produced a change of heart in Berlin, which reported, before the day was out, that 'On the subject of the members of the French forces who have been captured in the fighting at Bir Hacheim, no misunderstanding is possible. General de Gaulle's men will be treated as soldiers.'

Koenig's brigade regrouped at Sidi Barrani, where Catroux endeavoured to reinforce it. As the British withdrawal continued, the brigade fell back to El Alamein, where it was joined by General Cazaud and the 2nd Free French Brigade, as well as an armoured group commanded by Colonel Rémy. The Alsace fighter group, and the Lorraine bomber group assisted the RAF in the aerial combats over the Alamein position. Free French units continued to make long-range raids; a group under Captain Bergé destroyed twenty-one bombers, fifteen lorries and a petrol dump in Crete.

On 18th June, 1942, the second anniversary of his momentous appeal,

de Gaulle addressed a packed meeting in the Albert Hall. Behind the rostrum was a tricolour screen, bearing a huge Cross of Lorraine, the Free French badge. The general talked of the origins and recent history of Free France, and asserted that the movement was steadily gaining ground. 'When a ray of her reborn glory touched the bloodstained brows of her soldiers at Bir Hacheim', he thundered, 'the world recognised France.' Even the Germans recognised that Bir Hacheim signalled the resurgence of French fighting spirit. Captain Schmidt, of Rommel's staff, said of Koenig's garrison that 'theirs was the first sign of a revival of French fighting vitality since the débâcle of France in 1940.' Rommel, too, payed tribute to the French stand, remarking 'seldom in Africa was I given such a hard-fought struggle.' Von Mellenthin went even further and maintained that 'in the whole course of the desert war we never encountered a more heroic defence'.

The British High Command was, as one might expect, appreciative of

Generals Catroux, de Larminat and Koenig. 'Seldom in Africa was I given such a hard-fought struggle' (Rommel)

French tenacity. On 12th June Auchinleck declared that 'the United Nations owe it to themselves to be full of admiration and gratitude towards these French troops and their valiant general.' Three days later, Koenig issued a general order to his brigade.

'Officers, NCOs and men of the 1st Free French Brigade.

'You were entrusted with the task of defending Bir Hacheim, southern bastion of the Libyan defences.

'In fifteen days of almost uninterrupted fighting, you have wiped out important enemy forces, destroyed by gunfire fifty tanks, fifteen armoured cars, several vehicles of all types, shot down seventeen aircraft and captured in the course of your raids 154 Italian and 125 German prisoners.

'Enraged by our aggressive defence which foiled his plans, the enemy gradually increased the forces sent to exterminate you . . .

'Three times he ordered us to capitulate . . . But I had confidence in you. I answered the first demand by a polite but firm refusal. I did not even answer the other two, and the enemy made a fool of himself.

'When our task was completed, the General commanding the British Eighth Army ordered us to rejoin his army . . .

'Bir Hacheim is a French victory.

'I salute our dead, our brothers in arms killed in the fighting. The memory of them will sustain us in our future struggles.'

The acclaim which greeted the defence of Bir Hacheim could not conceal unpleasant suggestions from certain quarters that Free French morale had collapsed. Churchill referred to Koenig's withdrawal as 'a very heavy blow'. There were insinuations that the loss of Bir Hacheim was instrumental in causing the collapse of the Gazala Line and the fall of Tobruk. It is difficult to find evidence to sustain this argument. The breakout was sanctioned by the British High Command, and had been planned a day in advance;

it cannot, therefore, be described either as unauthorised or a last-minute panic measure. Koenig would, furthermore, have achieved little by remaining in position any longer. With the loss of Point 187, Bir Hacheim was, for all practical purposes, untenable. 150th Infantry Brigade at Sidi Muftah had fought, in Rommel's own words, 'to the last round of ammunition', but had been annihilated. It would have served little purpose for the Free French Brigade to have suffered a similar fate. Not only was Koenig's decision to breakout unquestionably correct, but the manoeuvre itself was carried out in a fashion which demonstrates the high morale of the garrison. The withdrawal was admittedly confused – but at no time did Koenig's men loose their fighting spirit. There were no scenes of alarm and panic such as had been all too common in 1940.

Bir Hacheim had held out longer than Ritchie had expected it to, and in doing so it had tied down increasing numbers of Axis troops. French possession of Bir Hacheim had endangered Rommel's tenuous line of supply, and presented Eighth Army with an excellent opportunity to cut off and destroy the *Panzerarmee*. The collapse of the Gazala Line, far from being due to the fall of Bir Hacheim, originated in errors at all levels of British command. Tanks were used in penny packets, armoured brigades being fed piecemeal into the German mincing-machine. Rommel's plan of attack was so ambitious as to be rash; but its manifest waeknesses were not exploited by the British. Ritchie, encumbered as he was by suggestions and directions from Churchill and Auchinleck, was unable to feel the pulse of the battle. His ripostes to Rommel's brisk jabs were weak and hesitant. The Gazala battles were, for the British, a tragic sequence of wasted time and lost opportunities.

Alexander inspects the justly proud Free French in October 1942

138

Towards liberation

While Free French forces in the Western Desert regrouped in the Alamein Line, the stirrings of resistance continued within France itself. The Resistance movement came into being slowly. De Gaulle's radio appeal of 18th June 1940 was heard by very few Frenchmen, though a repeat of the broadcast four days later had a larger audience. Isolated protests were made against German occupation; on 11th November 1940 numerous students gathered at the tomb of the unknown soldier in the Etoile, and were dispersed by German troops. In December, a young Frenchman was shot by firing-squad following an argument with a German soldier; the occupation was taking on a bitter tone. The early efforts of the Resistance were isolated, disorganised, and concerned largely with propaganda. A number of small Resistance groups sprang up, but the lack of cooperation between them limited their effectiveness, and made the task of the German security services considerably easier.

The British Special Operations Executive (SOE) gave substantial aid to the Resistance. SOE, however, did not always work in concert with the Free French BCRA, a fact which caused de Gaulle some chagrin. The general was further obstructed by the fact that many of the leaders of the Resistance had political outlooks which differed radically from his own. As time went on, the small Resistance organisations coalesced into larger groupings. In the north, for example, five main groups – *Ceux de la Liberation, Ceux de la Résistance, Front National, Liberation-Nord* and *L'Organisation Civile et Militaire* – crystallised out of many smaller bodies. *Front National*, with its militant arm, the *Francs-Tireurs Partisans*, was of Communist leanings, and was particularly strong in the 'Red Belt' around Paris. De Gaulle's main concern was to impose a degree of unity upon the Resistance movements, and subordinate them to his central control. This control was never more than symbolic.

In order to coordinate the activities of the Resistance, de Gaulle sent Jean Moulin to France. When war broke out, Moulin had been Prefect of *Eure et Loire* and Mayor of Chartres. After a period of imprisonment by the Germans, he escaped to Britain in September 1941. On the night of 1st January 1942, he was parachuted back into France as de Gaulle's 'Delegate-General'. Moulin's efforts met with considerable success; on 27th May 1943 the *Conseil National de la Résistance* was set up in Paris. Moulin himself was arrested only a few months later, and died in circumstances which remain unclear. His successor as Delegate-General, Jacques Bingen, fared little better, and committed suicide while in German hands. Bingen's replacement, too, was captured, and it was the fourth Delegate-General, Alexandre Parodi, who was to play such an important part in the liberation of Paris. During 1942 liaison between the Free French and the Resistance steadily improved. Some Resistance leaders – notably the socialists André Philip and Pierre Brossolette – came to London. Another notable arrival was Fernand Grenier, who, in January 1943, brought a message in which the French Communist Party gave Free France its full support.

By 1943 de Gaulle needed support wherever he could find it. Operation Torch, the Allied landings in North Africa in November 1942, had imperilled the Gaullist cause. This decline in de Gaulle's fortunes was due partly to the appearance of General Henri Giraud. Giraud had been captured by the Germans in May 1940, but had managed to escape, early in 1942, from incarceration in the fortress of Königstein. Giraud had then appeared at Vichy, and declared his support for the Pétain régime. He had little respect for either the Free French or the Resistance, and considered that the 100,000-man Armistice Army offered the most likely chance of ejecting the Germans from France. When con-

At El Alamein between 24th October and 4th November Rommel's troops were decisively defeated by Montgomery. Free French soldiers played an important part in the British victory, fighting at the southern end of the Alamein Line

Jean Moulin, sent by de Gaulle to France to coordinate the Resistance

tacted by American agents, Giraud urged that an Allied landing should be made in the south of France in the spring of 1943. Such a landing, he confidently maintained, would be supported by the Armistice Army.

The Allies, however, decided upon a landing in North Africa, and Giraud was ferried there by a British submarine. He arrived to find that French troops in Algeria and Morocco were offering strong resistance to Allied invasion forces. Fortunately, Pétain's heir-apparent, Admiral Darlan, happened to be in Algiers, and was persuaded to order a ceasefire. General Eisenhower, commanding the Allied forces, appointed Darlan political head of French North Africa; a questionable move, since the Admiral had collaborated with the Germans more thoroughly than most of his Vichy colleagues. Giraud was appointed Commander of French forces in Algeria and Morocco.

De Gaulle was enraged at the events in North Africa. He had not been consulted prior to the invasion, and considered that the Allies were making a deliberate attempt to replace him by

Giraud. This suspicion was, to an extent, justified. The Americans had little sympathy for de Gaulle; Roosevelt saw him as a man of great personal ambition, and the State Department mistrusted his dealings with the French Communist Party. American military interests also advocated de Gaulle's exclusion from the North African landings. Vichy resistance at Dakar and in Syria had, they argued, been directed primarily against the Free French, who should therefore be excluded from the North African venture. De Gaulle's relations with the British government had been going through a stormy period immediately prior to the landings. The general had declined a British suggestion that elections should be held in Syria and the Lebanon, and Churchill had responded by refusing to set up a Gaullist command in Madagascar. Some weeks later, on 6th November, the British proposed to de Gaulle that a joint communiqué should be issued, appointing General Legentilhomme High Commissioner in Madagascar. De Gaulle, rightly suspicious, feared that this was a minor concession to ensure French compliance while the Allies invaded North Africa. Two days later, Operation Torch was mounted.

German reaction to Torch was twofold. Hitler's troops poured into the unoccupied zone of southern France, encountering no resistance from the Armistice Army. The French fleet at Toulon failed to escape to North Africa, and scuttled itself rather than fall into German hands. In Africa itself, German soldiers were rushed into Tunisia at the rate of more than 1,000 a day. These forces were able to contain the Allies' eastward advance, but were of no help to Rommel's troops in the Western Desert, who were conclusively defeated by Montgomery at El Alamein between 24th October and 4th November. Free French soldiers played an important part in this British victory, fighting at the south of the Alamein Line.

In an atmosphere of growing

Maquisards, some of the more militant elements of the various Resistance movements which were combined into the *Forces Françaises de l'Intérieur* (the FFI) under Koenig. The FFI was, in effect, an underground army

General Legentilhomme, appointed High Commissioner in Madagascar

German-Italian friction, Rommel flew out to see Hitler, and pressed for a withdrawal into Tunisia. The Italians disagreed, and rightly distrusted offers of increased German support. Tripoli fell on 23rd January, and, although Rommel gave the Americans a bloody nose at the Kasserine Pass on 20th February, the situation continued to deteriorate for the Axis. Rommel hung onto his excellent position in the Mareth Line until 20th–26th March, when Montgomery at last ejected him. Instrumental in the Mareth Victory was General Leclerc's French force, which had earlier cleared the southern oases. Leclerc pushed through the 'Plum Pass', and fell on the German rear, doing considerable damage. Although Rommel managed to pull back with relatively small losses, the end in Africa was near. Rommel was ordered back to Germany, and his Italian successor withdrew on Enfida, which fell on 20th April. The strong Ras el Tib positions speedily collapsed, and on 12th May 250,000 Axis troops surrendered; so fell what General Jodl, German High Command, termed 'the glacis of Europe'.

Events, meanwhile, had been moving rapidly in Algiers. Darlan was assassinated on 25th December by Bonnier de la Chapelle, a young patriot who was shortly afterwards shot on Giraud's orders. The latter took over as Darlan's successor, and set about imprisoning or exiling Gaullist sympathisers. Giraud's régime was, in most respects, little different to that of Vichy. The ageing features of Marshal Pétain continued to adorn government offices, and Vichy legislation remained unaltered. Giraud maintained that victory over Germany should be the prime consideration; a French government was superfluous until France was liberated.

De Gaulle's position could not fail to be undermined by Giraud's power in North Africa. De Gaulle tried to arrange a meeting on unoccupied French territory, but Giraud vacillated. Churchill finally prevailed upon de Gaulle to visit Anfa, near Casablanca, where Roosevelt and he were in conference. Here de Gaulle met Giraud, but their reconciliation amounted simply to the two generals posing for a photograph showing them shaking hands. In an effort to unseat Giraud, de Gaulle was driven to the left. He stepped up negotiations with Russia, emphasising Giraud's 'dubious' past and the low fighting value of Vichy troops in North Africa. De Gaulle projected his own image as steadfastly anti-Vichy. Giraud, meanwhile, with his dictatorial legislation and anti-democratic methods, became more and more of an embarrassment to his American supporters. American efforts to democratise Giraud resulted in the general offending his adherent in North Africa by this unseemly change of heart. De Gaulle himself arrived in Algiers on 30th May, and commenced the final phase of the destruction of Giraud. The supporters of Giraud were dislodged from the Algiers Committee of National Liberation, and de Gaulle became its sole president. Giraud remained C-in-C, though, and in September managed to

Operation Torch, November 1942: the panzers (above) try desperately to hold back the Allied invasion which now includes Americans (below, a destroyed Stuart), but by 25th May the Axis troops are forced to surrender. General Leclerc's Free French played an important role in the Mareth victory

seize Corsica from its Axis garrison. This prestigious victory merely increased de Gaulle's determination to remove Giraud from the Algiers Committee altogether, a task which he accomplished a few months later.

The defeat of Giraud enabled de Gaulle to de-radicalise, and somewhat soften his attitude towards Vichyites, a fact which pleased the Americans. As Giraud's former adherents changed their allegiance to de Gaulle, the military strength of Free France – or, to give it its new title, Fighting France – increased. By the beginning of 1944 there were about 400,000 French troops supporting the Allied cause; strangely enough, most of these soldiers had originally been Vichyite rather than Free French.

General Juin's 120,000-man French force was engaged in Sicily and Italy, and demonstrated the same fighting spirit which had distinguished French troops in the desert. In France itself, the Resistance was organised even more tightly than before. The militant

General Henri Giraud, appointed to command French forces in Algeria and Morocco

elements of the various Resistance movements were combined into the *Forces Françaises de l'Interieur*, under the command of the bold Koenig. The FFI was, in effect, an underground army. It was organised on a hierarchical basis, with a fabric of regional commands and military ranks which made the issue of orders and the declineation of responsibility much clearer. There were, inevitably, hitches. The communists tended to have a deep-seated dislike for conventional military organisations. At the other extreme, disputes arose in the provinces as to how many *galons* (officer's stripes) local Resistance leaders were to have. Koenig was recognised as commander of the FFI by Supreme HQ, Allied Expeditionary Force (SHAEF), on 30th May 1944. He was to be assisted by tripartite inter-Allied staff, headed by a French Chief of

Jacques Soustelle, head of the DGSS which coordinated all the secret organisations in France

General Juin, commander of the 120,000-man French force fighting in Sicily and Italy

Staff. These arrangements were approved by the Algiers Committee, and implemented in a document drawn up by SHAEF on 17th June. Koenig eventually had two Chiefs of Staff. Colonel de Chevigné was in charge of military operations, and the ubiquitous Passy supervised relations with France. Passy had left BCRA in March 1944 after repeated disputes with d'Astier de la Vigerie, *commissaire* for the Interior.

All secret organisations were coordinated by the *Direction Generale des Services Speciaux*, (DGSS), under Jacques Soustelle. Soustelle was a remarkable individual. He had obtained his degree at the early age of twenty, and his doctorate five years later. While in Mexico, studying Mayan civilisation, he developed the theory that national destiny could be altered by the efforts of an individual. He joined the Free French in 1940, and remained a steadfast supporter of de Gaulle. Soustelle's organisation had two branches, one in Algiers and the other in London. The latter achieved great importance, sifting and circulating reports from occupied France.

As the date of the Normandy landings approached, there remained several points of friction between de Gaulle and the Allies. Until the agreement with SHAEF in May, Koenig was kept very much in the dark as to the invasion plan. And, though the Americans had now dropped the unpalatable Giraud, Roosevelt maintained a disturbing attitude towards any possible French government. 'I am not able to recognise any government of France', he warned, 'until the people of France have an opportunity to make a free choice.'

Sabotage. Throughout 1943 the maquis was growing in numbers and skill ...

This naturally led to fears that France might be subjected, as Italy had been, to Allied Military Government of Occupied Territory (AMGOT). To forestall any attempts to set up an Allied Military Government, or, indeed, a puppet French government, the Algiers Committee declared itself, on 3rd June, three days before D-Day, the provisional government of France. It was not, however, recognised as such by the Allies for some considerable time. It was, therefore, essential for de Gaulle to demonstrate as soon as possible that France recognised him as her leader.

There remained the problem of the Resistance. This had become increasingly subject to Communist influence, and considerable efforts would be required to persuade it to conform to Gaullist authority following a successful invasion. A new military hierarchy, with national, zonal and regional military delegates, was superimposed upon the existing, often Communist-infiltrated, command structure. Although this made the chain of command complex, it increased the possibility of central control in a post-liberation situation.

The Normandy landings were preceded by a dispute between de Gaulle and Churchill as to the Free French rôle in the operation. Churchill hoped that de Gaulle would broadcast to the French people on D-Day. De Gaulle, though, objected; the speeches of Churchill and Eisenhower had been pre-recorded, and did not include instructions that the French should obey only the Gaullists. Finally, de Gaulle did agree to broadcast, and in the course of his speech demanded obedience to his own organisation. Free French military participation in the invasion was small. A Commando Company landed with the British at Ouistreham, and another group was parachuted into the central region of Brittany. Units of the Free French navy also assisted the invasion.

If the efforts of regular Free French forces were limited, the same could not be said of those of the FFI. A series of detailed sabotage plans had been drawn up, dealing with all facilities that might prove useful to the Wehrmacht. *Plan Vert* dealt with the railways, *Plan Bleu* with electricity supplies, and so on. Particular attention was paid to bridges and road junctions which it would be difficult or costly for Allied bombers to reach. The sabotage programme proved brilliantly successful. French saboteurs and Allied aircraft cut Normandy off from the rest of France, and dislocated German communications. German reinforcements were slowed up; it took 11th Panzer Division a week to get from the Eastern Front to the Rhine, and three weeks to get from the Rhine to the Caen front. The élite SS Panzer Division 'Das Reich' was held up for a fortnight by partisan action in the Dordogne. When its heavy elements tried to bypass the trouble spots by rail, they were promptly destroyed from the air.

On 10th June Koenig warned his forces not to launch large-scale operations prematurely. Several major actions were, however, fought by the FFI. At Mont-Mouchet, near Clermont-Ferrand, a body of over 3,000 maquisards inflicted some 3,000 casualties on the Germans. In the Vercours, a *massif* lying between Die and Grenoble, a *maquis* unit held out for a considerable time against German assaults, but was finally overrun with the loss of about 1,000 men. Both these operations were based on misunderstandings; Allied assistance, in the shape of heavy equipment and paratroops, was wrongly believed to be on the way.

De Gaulle's provisional government remained unrecognised, and for a time the general himself was stranded in Britain. Between 8th-30th June several of the governments-in-exile – Belgian, Polish, Norwegian, Yugoslavian and Czechoslovakian – acknowledged de Gaulle's provisional government. It was not until a week after D-Day that de Gaulle managed to get to France, aboard the French destroyer *La Combattante*. He paid a short visit to

. . . by early 1944 it posed a serious threat to Germany's war effort

Bayeux, and appointed Francois Coulet *Commissaire de la Republique* for Normandy. The anti-Gaullist outburst which Roosevelt had so gloomily predicted was not forthcoming. Local Vichy authorities were only too glad to submit to de Gaulle's representatives. The general himself remained in France for only a few hours, and then returned to London. He shortly afterwards travelled to Washington, by way of Rome and Algiers. In Washington, his meeting with the American President went, as might be expected, rather badly. Although Roosevelt was much better disposed towards de Gaulle than he had been on previous occasions, the general found American ideas of postwar 'spheres of influence' abhorrent.

In Normandy, the battle raged. The German High Command had been uncertain as to the probable direction of the Allied assault, and had concentrated many of its divisions in the Pas de Calais area. The landings began on the morning of 6th June; the bridgeheads were linked up by 11th June. Cherbourg fell on 27th June, and there was severe fighting around Caen, which was seized on 9th July. General Patton's American Third Army surged

into Brittany from the broadening bridgehead. A German counterattack, launched in obedience to Hitler's demented strategy, was held and outflanked, and the resultant battle of the Falaise pocket crippled the German Fifth Panzer and Seventh Armies.

In Paris, for so long prostrate beneath German rule, the population became increasingly aware of the approach of the Allies. A growing disorganisation among the occupying forces also became apparent. A portly Saxon, General Dietrich von Choltitz, replaced General von Stülpnagel as Commandant of Paris. Stülpnagel himself had been involved in the abortive 20th July bomb plot against Hitler, and was in hospital following an unsuccessful suicide attempt. Von Choltitz visited Hitler's HQ at Rastenburg in East Prussia, and received uncompromising orders to hold Paris to the last. The FFI had other ideas. Colonel René Tanguy – known as Colonel Rol – commander of the FFI in the *Ile de France*, advocated an, insurrection within Paris, to wrest the

D-Day. The Free French (right) played only a minor role, but the FFI was sabotaging incessantly

city from the Germans before the Allies arrived. De Gaulle's representatives, Parodi and Chaban-Delmas, were less convinced of the wisdom of 'direct action'. From de Gaulle's viewpoint, however, it was essential that Paris should be liberated, if not by the FFI from within, then by Free French forces from without.

The means for a Free French liberation of Paris were, fortunately, at hand. General Philippe Leclerc's 2nd Armoured Division had landed in France on 1st August, and had been engaged near Mortain. In the south, Operation Anvil – landings on the Riviera – had proceeded successfully, and General Jean de Lattre de Tassigny's First French Army was among the Allied forces involved. It was Leclerc's division, though, which was chosen by the American General Omar Bradley for the honour of entry into Paris, a decision which suited de Gaulle perfectly. Nonetheless, hazards still remained. One of de Gaulle's fears was that the tireless Laval would succeed in establishing a 'National Government', claiming legal continuity from the Third Republic. Between 9th-17th August, Laval did indeed try this last, desperate throw, striving to persuade Edouard Herriot, President of the Chamber, to summon the Assembly. Herriot refused, and was arrested by the Germans; both Laval and Pétain were taken to Germany. Thus passed the well-intentioned but misguided Vichy régime.

The removal of Laval and Pétain worked very much in de Gaulle's favour. The collapse of Vichy left a political vacuum within France, a vacuum which only de Gaulle was now in a position to fill. Leclerc's Shermans rumbled towards Paris, and de Gaulle waited at Eisenhower's HQ for the liberation of the city. Within Paris, the situation became increasingly hectic. German troops withdrew by road and rail, and the activities of the Resistance increased to fever-pitch. Von Choltitz received orders from Berlin to destroy the city

if its capture was inevitable, but he informed the French Prefect of Police that he had no intention of acting against the population unless they made the first move. Von Choltitz had no wish to destroy the city or to kill its inhabitants; he was concerned to hold out long enough to satisfy military honour and to surrender to Allied regular forces. Resistance leaders met to finalise their plans, with Parodi making every effort to ensure Gaullist domination of the coming rising. On 19th August, the Resistance struck. Holding various key points within the city, they fired on von Choltitz's troops, who responded somewhat half-heartedly. The Swedish Consul-General, Raoul Nordling, negotiated a temporary truce during which many French prisoners were freed, but the fighting swelled up again on the 22nd. Two days later, on the evening of 24th August, the advance guard of Leclerc's division entered Paris.

The main body of 2nd Armoured Division clattered into Paris on 25th August. Von Choltitz was captured at his HQ and taken to the command post of one of Leclerc's colonels, where the surrender of Paris was signed. The fighting ended as night fell. De Gaulle had arrived in Paris at about 1600 hours. He decided not to go straight to the *Hôtel de Ville*, where the *Conseil National de la Résistance* was in session, but went instead to Leclerc's HQ at the *Gare Montparnasse*. This clearly reveals de Gaulle's determination to avoid being 'invested' with power by the Resistance. Furthermore, a proclamation issued by the CNR that day had referred to the provisional government, but not to the general personally – another cause for Gaullist picque. It was not until after he had established himself in his old office at the Ministry of War in the Rue St-Dominque that de Gaulle went to the *Hôtel de Ville*, and then only after visiting the Police Prefecture en route Once at the *Hotel de Ville*, de Gaulle

Ordre pour la défense de la Population Parisienne

Les F. F. I. et la population ont engagé la bataille pour PARIS. Chaque fois que nos soldats ont respecté la tactique mobile de la guérilla, ils ont écrasé l'adversaire

Cependant, un danger subsiste : les mouvements rapides des chars ennemis.

Ce danger est facile à conjurer.

Il suffit d'empêcher les boches de rouler.

Pour cela, que toute la Population parisienne, Hommes, Femmes, Enfants, construisent des barricades, que tous abattent des arbres sur les Avenues, Boulevards et Grandes Rues.

Que toutes les petites rues soient partiellement obstruées par des barricades en chicanes.

Organisez-vous, par maison et par rue pour garantir votre défense contre toute attaque ennemie.

Dans ces conditions, le boche sera isolé et cerné dans quelques centres, **il ne pourra plus exercer de représailles.**

TOUS AUX BARRICADES !

Le Colonel, Chef du Grand PARIS : **ROL.**

AVIS

Le couvre-feu est primé à dater du 22 AOUT 1944 et jusqu'à nouvel ordre.

Les portes des immeubles doivent être ouvertes aux combattants français et fermées aux boches sous peine de sanctions graves.

Le camouflage des lumières reste obligatoire.

Le Colonel, Chef du Grand PARIS : **ROL.**

Above : The appeal by Colonel Rol (otherwise known as René Tanguy, commandor of the FFI In the *Ile de France*) for the Parisians to wrest Paris from the Germans. *Below :* Insurrectionists fire from the windows of the *Hôtel de Ville*

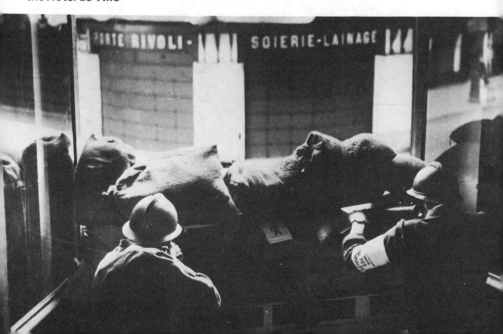

made a speech which failed to mention the Resistance or the CNR, dwelling largely on 'national unity' and the continued need for victory over Germany. He declined a suggestion that he follow tradition by proclaiming the Republic from the balcony of the *Hôtel de Ville*, replying; 'The Republic has never ceased to exist . . . Vichy was, and remains, nothing. I am the President of the Government of the Republic. Why should I proclaim it?'

On Saturday, 26th August, de Gaulle made his triumphal procession across Paris. Witnesses described the scene as more dramatic, even, than the victory parade of 1919. De Gaulle strode down the *Champs-Elysées*, followed by the men who had made that day possible; Parodi, Juin, Leclerc and Koenig. The crowds were delirious with enthusiasm, surging in wild excitement on either side of the road. Having crossed the *Place de la Concorde*, de Gaulle entered a car which took him to Notre-Dame. Here he was greeted by similar scenes of excitement – and by a scattered salvo of shots, to which he paid no attention. It has not been established who was responsible for this shooting, though it seems unlikely that the general was the target. De Gaulle set great store by his enthusiastic reception by, according to his own account, 2,000,000 Parisians. This in itself was a form of investiture, carrying, in the general's view, infinitely more weight than any given by the CNR.

The painful fact that the war was not yet over was vividly demonstrated by the Luftwaffe, which delivered a particularly savage air raid on Paris on the night of 26th August. General de Lattre de Tassigny's army was in action near Grenoble, and many members of the FFI from liberated areas were eager to join in the fighting. Of the 250,000 men making up First French Army in the battles in Lorraine, 137,000 were members of the FFI. Two weeks after the liberation of Paris, de Gaulle formed a reconstituted administration, the Government of 'National Unanimity'. It contained many of the members of the provisional government, and some of de Gaulle's original London team. No members of this administration were connected with Vichy.

Left : The response to Colonel Rol's appeal — the construction of barricades in Paris. *Above :* A week after D-Day, de Gaulle received a tumultuous welcome in Bayeux. *Below :* Place de la Concorde, 24th August

Such national unanimity as existed did not long survive the war's conclusion. De Gaulle's friction with the left-wing elements of the Resistance continued. The war had left the French army more heterogeneous than ever. It included veterans who had been with the Free French since the beginning, young FFI officers, often holding high ranks but with little conventional military training, and, finally, the *napthalinés*, Vichy officers who had emerged from retirement in uniforms redolent of mothballs. The inevitable postwar reductions in the armed forces produced much bitterness among those whose military careers were prematurely terminated. Three times in 1945 France's new army tramped down the *Champs-Elysées*, past crowds whose enthusiasm seemed, alas, to wane on each successive occasion. In the same way that the victory parade of 1919 had obscured sordid realities, so the parades of 1945 could veil only dimly France's uncertain future. But whatever the future might hold, it was, at least, filled with hope. France had emerged from the war not without honour. The disaster of 1940 and the sad tale of Vichy and collaboration were not the whole story. France had made a brave and effective contribution towards her own liberation.

The history of the Free French movement is full of moments of gloom and despair, but at no time did de Gaulle lose confidence in an ultimate Allied victory. The military fortunes of Free France, too, had fluctuated, but French soldiers had shown that, well led and convinced in the cause for which they fought, they were more than a match for the same forces which had so ignominiously routed them in 1940. In the last analysis, Bir Hacheim is an important turning-point in the history of Free France. Bir Hacheim was not the beginning of the end, but it was, to paraphrase Churchill, the end of the beginning.

2,000,000 Parisians welcome de Gaulle

Bibliography

Bir Hakeim by Felix de Grand'combef (Tresses Universitaires de France)
History of the Second World War, Volume 3 by Barrie Pitt (ed) (Purnell, London)
The Foxes of the Desert by Paul Carrell (Macdonald, London)
The Mediterranean and the Middle East, Volume 3 by ISO Playfair (HMSO, London)
Tobruk by Michael Carver (Batsford)
With Rommel in the Desert by Heinz Werner Schmidt (Harrap, London)